MW01069081

San Elizario
Spanish Presidio to Texas County Seat

San Elizario
Spanish Presidio to Texas County Seat

by Rick Hendricks and W. H. Timmons

Texas Western Press

The University of Texas at El Paso
1998

First Edition
Library of Congress Catalog No. 96-61729
ISBN 0-87404-242-9

∞ Texas Western Press books are printed on acid-free paper, meeting the guidelines for permanence and durability of the Committee on Production Guidelines for Book Longevity of the Council on Library Resources.

Cover art and text illustrations by José Cisneros

*Texas Western Press gratefully
acknowledges the dedicated support
Mr. Cisneros has given over the many years of his association
with this Press and in particular,
the beautiful drawings that grace this volume.*

Contents

PREFACE

The presidio of San Elizario was one of the last to be constructed on New Spain's northern frontier with building getting under way in 1789 and continuing for a number of years. It was also among the last to serve the Mexican Republic, soldiering on until United States troops overran the area in 1846. We would argue, moreover, that the presidio of San Elizario was one of the most important, particularly for its role as both active military post and administrator of Apache peace camps. The town that emerged from the shadow of the presidio was of no less importance, twice serving as El Paso County seat before losing out to upstart Anglo El Paso. As with the presidio, the documents that constitute what is called the Juárez Archive, the two microfilm collections of the documentary repository in neighboring Ciudad Juárez, which were prepared by the University of Texas at El Paso, reveal much about the town of San Elizario and the transformation of these basic frontier institutions.

A large part of this study is drawn from sources that have never been consulted before in this context and for this end. We have, therefore, made what we believe to be a judicious selection of representative documents and translated them for inclusion in a documentary appendix. We have also drawn on coauthor W.H. Timmons's previous scholarship, occasionally quoting from his work in chapter three. Because El Paso almost totally eclipses San Elizario in the documentary record for the period it covers, chapter four relies on and quotes liberally from his *El Paso: A Borderlands History* (1990).

The mission, the town, and the presidio (a term used to describe both a frontier garrison and the fortification in which soldiers served) have long been considered the fundamental institutions of Spain's empire in the Americas.[1] Two decades have passed since the publication of Max L. Moorhead's *The Presidio: Bastion of the Spanish Borderlands* (1975). Two volumes edited by Thomas H. Naylor and Charles W. Polzer, S.J., of the Documentary Relations of the Southwest at the University of Arizona, *The Presidio and Militia on the Northern Frontier of New Spain, 1570-1700* (1986) and *Pedro de Rivera and the Military Regulations for Northern New Spain, 1724-1729* (1988), have added greatly to our knowledge of the presidio as an institution. William B. Griffen's anthropological examination of Apaches at the presidio of Janos in the Spanish and Mexican periods, *Apaches at War and Peace: The Janos Presidio, 1750-1858* (1988), has provided insight into the workings of a single presidio and challenged others to undertake similar studies. Within the last decade, one Texas presidio has been carefully scrutinized; three studies—two in the United States and one in Mexico—have dealt with various aspects of the history of the presidial and mission community of San Antonio de Béxar, including the recently published *San Antonio de Béxar: A Community on New Spain's Northern Frontier* (1995), by Jesús F. de la Teja. In addition, numerous other books and articles have added breadth and depth to the study of the presidio, as have ongoing archaeological investigations at several California sites, such as the San Diego and San Francisco presidios.

Important advances such as these notwithstanding, remarkably little is known about most of the individual presidios that dotted the frontier. With respect to the presidio of San Elizario[2] and the community that grew out of it, in particular, beyond Eugene O. Porter's *San Elizario: A History* (1973), a brief, popular treatment, and several obscure articles by the authors of this study, its history remains largely unwritten. This is the result in large measure of the fact that the early history of the presidio and community of San Elizario lay undetected or overlooked for many years in the documents of the Juárez Archive. Recent research in Mexican and Spanish archival material has complemented this rich, little-used documentation, and now the story can be told.

The reader should note that we have modernized the spelling of Spanish names; thus we refer to Viceroy Manuel Antonio Flores, even though he always signed Florez. We have used *Webster's New Geographical Dictionary* as our guide for place-names; hence Cadiz appears without

an accent. Following *Webster's Third New International Dictionary of the English Language Unabridged*, words such as alferez and rancheria, which are accented in Spanish, are now accepted as English words of Spanish origin and written without accents.

This book would be much the poorer and our interpretations much different were it not for the cooperation of our Mexican and Spanish colleagues. In particular, we would like to express our appreciation to Enrique Cervantes at the Archivo General de la Nación in Mexico City for facilitating access to uncatalogued material from Caja Matriz and Guerra y Marina and to Francisco Javier Alvarez Pinedo at the Archivo General de Simancas for working with us to provide much-needed documentation on service records of men who served at the presidio of San Elizario. Closer to home, we wish to thank Lois Stanford, William Hendricks, Laura Timmons, and Constance and Albert Hulbert for lovingly encouraging and indulging us at monthly lunches during the last several years as this book took shape. Nancy Hamilton and Meredith D. Dodge read the entire manuscript and offered numerous suggestions for its improvement, as did two anonymous readers. Marta Estrada of San Elizario shared her newspaper clipping file.

Finally, we would like to thank Samuel Sánchez, Sr., of Clint, Texas, for graciously providing from his family papers a copy of a land grant to Mateo Montes (that mentions Sánchez's relative, Mariano Alvarado), for it is the only one of its kind we have found and a valued link to the past we feel privileged to share.[3]

Rick Hendricks
Las Cruces, New Mexico
W. H. Timmons
El Paso, Texas

INTRODUCTION

When they arrived at the abandoned site of Los Tiburcios early in 1789, the men of the presidio of San Elizario and their families may well have had mixed emotions. There could be no denying that, as the military strategists had noted, there was everything needed for a prosperous settlement: cleared fields of rich, alluvial soil; an acequia (ditch irrigation) system; and an ample supply of timber. Nevertheless, there was no one there. Simply put, Los Tiburcios had been too isolated from the other riverine communities that stretched south and east downriver from El Paso del Norte, exposed to marauding Apaches who had recently stepped up the tempo of their raiding. It would have been clear to the newly arrived troops that the area had once been an extensive ranching complex.

Until documents recently surfaced, we had only the vaguest of ideas about the nature of the settlement at Los Tiburcios. The name had first appeared on fray Miguel de Menchero's 1744 map of New Mexico. Now it is possible to trace its history in some detail, and we have attempted to do so in chapter one. A verbatim copy extracted from the original purchase agreement in the opening decades of the eighteenth century enabled us to locate the properties belonging to the ranch of Nuestra Señora de la Soledad de Los Tiburcios and gain some understanding of the scale of its operations. Sacramental records and wills from the area made it possible to connect many of the individuals who together formed a family operation that, at its peak, involved more than two hundred people.

It has long been assumed that the presidio of San Elizario was relocated to Los Tiburcios as a bastion of defense to protect wayfarers moving up and down the human highway that was the camino real. This, despite the fact that the presidio was at the end of a spur road and not astride the camino real proper. While the presidio routinely provided escort for travelers and goods, that was not its primary role. The documentary evidence, which we present in chapter two, roundly refutes this assumption on two counts. First, there is no doubt that the choice of Los Tiburcios as the new site for the presidio of San Elizario had everything to do with its suitability for administering Apache peace camps and little to do with defense of the El Paso area. El Paso's own presidial company had been shifted to Carrizal in 1773 because the villa was large enough to protect itself with reorganized militia units. Second, the mounted company of the presidio of San Elizario did not adopt a defensive posture. While peace was granted to those Apache rancherias that requested it, a sizable contingent of presidial troops was almost constantly in the field to wage aggressive war against those Apaches who refused to accept the proffered peace.

Much of this chapter is devoted to describing the Apache peace program as it was conducted at San Elizario. Records for San Elizario comparable to those William B. Griffen found at Janos have not surfaced. For that reason, we have been unable to construct a parallel statistical study of the manner in which the program was administered at the presidio of San Elizario. In addition, there are notable lacunae in the record. What remains, however, weaves a rich tapestry that unfolds in the voluminous official correspondence from which we have constructed a narrative history of the Apache peace program and the life of the presidio during the late eighteenth and early nineteenth centuries.

Two related themes develop in the third chapter: the transition of the presidio from a Spanish imperial to a Mexican national institution and the emergence of the Mexican town of San Elizario. Administrative reform growing out of nation building, such as the redrawing of jurisdictions, played itself out in San Elizario just as it did all along Mexico's northern frontier. All the El Paso area communities soon passed from New Mexico to the state of Chihuahua.

Newly uncovered documents, the result of research in Mexican and Spanish archival collections, shed considerable light on the transition of the presidio from Spanish administration to Mexican control. From legislation and service records of presidial soldiers, it seems clear that during the turbulent struggle for independence, some chose to fight for Spain and others—probably most—opted to defend the new nation, Mexico, which had arisen from their native New Spain. In the years immediately after Mexican independence, major legislation sought to reorganize the presidial system. On paper, at least, the new nation recognized the effectiveness of the presidios and budgeted hefty sums to keep large complements of troops on hand at a number of presidios, including San Elizario. In practice, the record is equally clear that as early as the twilight years of Spanish rule, many of the presidial troops from San Elizario were often on assignment elsewhere, most notably in New Mexico, on escort duty, putting down a rebellion, or preparing to repel invading Texans. Throughout this period, the presidio continued its relationship with the Apaches, at some times in battle and at others administering an on-again-off-again peace program.

More remarkable than the relatively smooth transition to Mexican control of the presidio was the emergence of the town of San Elizario as the dominant institution. As the presidial troops played an ever-increasing role in the affairs of neighboring New Mexico, the citizens of San Elizario took steps to provide for their own defense. Of particular interest are documents that demonstrate how the people of San Elizario faced the rise of the Lone Star Republic. Local citizens contributed money from their meager resources and passed muster in a demonstration of their willingness to defend their town against the hated Texans.

When most of the presidial troops joined an expeditionary force to New Mexico in 1843, the citizenry of San Elizario was left largely to its own devices. Even though the expected invasion never reached Santa Fe, the troops from San Elizario assigned there remained. In 1845 El Paso area towns were on a war footing; that spring only five soldiers from San Elizario were in the region. When United States forces occupied the area after the defeat of Mexican forces at the Battle of Brazito in December 1846, they found only the remnants of their vanquished foe and an obese priest at the presidio of San Elizario. The presidio had figuratively and literally begun to disappear. With its troops often on assignment elsewhere, it had lost much of its importance to the town as an institution. As for its massive walls, the citizens had also begun to dismantle them, carrying off the adobes to be reused in other construction.

The Treaty of Guadalupe Hidalgo ended the war between the United States and Mexico in February 1848, fixing the local international boundary as the deepest channel of the Rio Grande. American officials argued that the southern channel was the deepest one and that there-fore Ysleta, Socorro, and the presidio of San Elizario were in United States territory. United States troops occupied the area shortly thereafter. With stunning suddenness, a community firmly rooted in Spanish-Mexican traditions and culture became part of a very different country. Remarkably, just over one year later, San Elizario was selected county seat of newly formed El Paso County. San Elizario, it seemed, was on its way. With a population of some 1,200, the growing town was poised to lead the area for the foreseeable future. Following a stagnant period during the Civil War, however, newly arrived Anglo-Americans centered in El Paso quickly came to dominate the entire area. San Elizario, peopled largely by poorer Mexican-Americans, soon lost influence, although it continued to lead in population. This decline culminated in 1873 when an election approved the relocation of the county seat to Ysleta. The fate of San Elizario—relegated to a diminished role in local affairs—was sealed in 1881 when the railroad arrived, bypassing the town in favor of El Paso. This change was not unwelcome, however, for it enabled San Elizario to preserve its essentially rural character. The flood of 1897 delivered a truly devastating and entirely unwelcome blow from which San Elizario never really recovered. This abrupt transition, rapid ascendancy, and decline are related in chapter four.

The documentary appendix consists of seven items: the first inspection of the relocated presidio of San Elizario

(1790), the service record of a Spanish presidial soldier (1790), Pedro de Nava's instructions for dealing with Apaches at peace in Nueva Vizcaya (1791), a Spanish land grant (1803), a Mexican muster of the presidial company (1836), the service record of a soldier who served under Spain and Mexico (1842), and a list of citizens for the Texas campaign (1846).

THE NORTHERN FRONTIER OF NEW SPAIN IN THE LATE EIGHTEENTH CENTURY

THE INTERIOR PROVINCES

THE INTERIOR PROVINCES

Charles III, who ascended the throne of Spain in 1759, was the most empire-minded monarch since Philip II in the latter half of the sixteenth century. His rule of twenty-nine years was largely dedicated to the unceasing demands of colonial and international affairs. On his assumption of the throne, in addition to the perennial problem of Apache raids on the northern frontier of the Viceroyalty of New Spain, there was the European international situation. The Treaty of Paris of 1763 at the close of the Seven Years' War forced Spain to cede Florida to Great Britain in order to recover Havana and Manila, which it had lost to British forces during the war. Thus Great Britain, Spain's traditional rival, held all the territory east of the Mississippi River. Moreover, the treaty removed Spain's ally France from North America, for Spain received all French territory west of the Mississippi River and retained it until 1821. The northern frontier of the Viceroyalty of New Spain thus remained a primary concern of Spanish monarchs for more than half a century, particularly in the period after 1803 when the United States purchased the Louisiana territory.[1]

In 1765 Charles III sent the eminent José de Gálvez to New Spain with the title of *visitador general* and authority to institute sweeping reforms in the administration of the viceroyalty. In that same year, and as part of the same reorganization, the king appointed the Marqués de Rubí to inspect all the presidios on the northern frontier of the viceroyalty and submit whatever recommendations he thought necessary for the improvement of the system. Nicolás de Lafora, captain of the Spanish Royal Engineers, was assigned to accompany Rubí for the purpose of mapping and describing the region visited. The result was a day-by-day narrative of the journey, which lasted twenty-three months and covered almost 3,000 leagues, or more than 7,600 miles. On his return to Mexico City in February 1768, Rubí completed his celebrated *Dictamen*, or general assessment of the situation on the frontier. His basic recommendation was a single cordon of presidios—possibly fifteen—spaced about forty leagues (a hundred miles) apart that could halt any invasion of the interior.[2]

Rubí noted in his *Dictamen* that since the El Paso complex with its 5,000 souls was the largest in the Interior Provinces, it could provide its own defense. The El Paso presidio should then be removed from New Mexico to Carrizal, in the jurisdiction of Nueva Vizcaya. Another Rubí recommendation—one that would relate to the El Paso area in the future—was that the presidio of Guajoquilla, near present-day Jiménez, Chihuahua, should be moved to the valley of San Elceario on the banks of the Rio Grande. The Spanish crown subsequently incorporated Rubí's recommendations into one of the most significant documents in Spanish Borderlands history—The Royal Regulations of 1772.[3]

In 1772 Lieutenant Colonel Hugo O'Conor, a Spanish official born in Dublin, Ireland, with seven years' experience in Texas, was named to the post of inspector-general of the Interior Provinces. His task was twofold: relocate the presidios in keeping with the Rubí recommendations and organize an all-out campaign against the Apaches. During the next three years O'Conor traveled ten thousand miles in an attempt to carry out his assigned tasks. Some of the older sites were abandoned; others were established; and several were transferred, such as El Paso del Norte to Carrizal. His efforts to launch an attack against the Apaches in the Bolsón de Mapimí, in which he hoped to utilize forces to be supplied by the governors of Texas, Coahuila, and New Mexico, fell short of desired objectives. His failure was largely the result of inadequate planning, faulty coordination, and shortages of supplies, personnel, firearms, and mounts. A disappointed, frustrated O'Conor asked to be relieved of his position, citing declining health as the reason, and late in 1776 his request was granted. He died three years later at the age of forty-five.[4]

Since it was readily apparent that the Rubí recommendations and the resulting Royal Regulations of 1772 had not yet solved the Apache problem, the Spanish crown in

1776 established the office of commandant general of the Interior Provinces, with powers virtually equal to those of a viceroy. An officer of exceptional intelligence, energy, and ability, the French-born Teodoro de Croix, was named to this new frontier office.[5]

Croix believed in a military solution to the Indian problem, as had Rubí and O'Conor before him. In a series of war councils, general strategy was agreed upon. This consisted of a provincial governor's campaign against the eastern Apaches involving a force of three thousand men; an investigation of the possibility of a Spanish-Comanche alliance; an increase in presidial complements by some 1,800 or more; the creation of provincial militias and *compañías volantes*, or mobile companies, quick-striking, hard-hitting forces; and the use of "light troops," units that had been relieved of the heavy jackets and equipment.[6]

In July 1779, however, just as Croix's offensive was beginning to gain momentum, the Spanish crown announced a startling new development, its imminent declaration of war on Great Britain. Croix was therefore ordered to reduce his own expenditures, cease all operations against the hostiles, make an attempt to conciliate them by peaceful persuasion, and confine his own activities to purely defensive measures. Thus the aggressive Indian policy Rubí had first recommended, which had been consistently pursued since 1768, had now been drastically reversed by the Spanish crown. Croix's dream of a war of extermination from the Gulf of Mexico to the Gulf of California had been completely shattered.[7]

A disappointed but obedient Croix nevertheless decided that he must carry on. Obviously he would have to revise his planning and adopt a defensive pattern. He first moved his headquarters to Arizpe, Sonora, an indication that California was gaining importance in Spanish frontier strategy. During the next four years he was able to achieve some degree of success in stabilizing the Indian problem. He relocated some presidios and established several new ones, made his system of mobile companies more effective, built a second line of defense with organizations such as the Provincial Corps of Nueva Vizcaya, reorganized a number of local militias, and signed peace terms with the Comanches of New Mexico. For services rendered, the Spanish crown rewarded him in 1783 with the prestigious post of viceroy of Peru.[8]

THE APACHES

With the beginning of the eighteenth century a new and far greater problem than any yet experienced by the hardy settlers of the El Paso area had emerged—a nomadic and predatory group known as the Apaches. The land they inhabited—the Gran Apachería, as the Spaniards sometimes called it—stretched from the Texas Panhandle to the Rio Grande Valley and westward to the Arizona desert. Their main range was the desert Southwest, though they could extend their murderous raids, for either plunder or revenge, deep into what is now northern Mexico. Hostilities between Apache and Spaniard thus became a major theme in the area for a century and a half, and the settlers of El Paso del Norte and the surrounding area, time and again were the victims of relentless, destructive Apache raids and depredations.[9]

Although many tribes and subtribes were affiliated with the Apaches, by far the most troublesome for the El Paso settlers were the Gileños west of the Rio Grande, the Faraones in southern New Mexico, and the Mescaleros east of the Rio Grande. These groups had traditionally lived off the buffalo, but during the eighteenth century under increasing Comanche pressure, they became a greater threat to settlements everywhere on the northern frontier. Their principal target was livestock, since they considered the flesh of horses and mules the sweetest and tastiest of meats, and they would go to any length to obtain it, destroying anyone who stood in their way. They chose the highest lookout points to appraise a situation but rarely attacked if they suspected superior numbers. Their style of fighting was to raid and plunder small towns and ranches, murder the inhabitants, carry off the children, and drive off the horses and cattle. Mounted on fleet ponies, capable of performing incredible feats of marksmanship with the bow and arrow and the lance, the Apaches learned to strike fast, stay out of range of Spanish muzzle-loaders, burn, pillage, ambush, retreat, and scatter, thus making them a formidable foe, who was virtually impossible to control. They used smoke signals to warn of the approach of soldiers and would then retreat to mountainous areas the troops found impenetrable. For an entire century and a half the Apaches kept the residents of frontier communities in a continual state of terror, since it was difficult to predict when these "Mongols of the desert" would strike or in what numbers.[10]

The Apache groups viewed the vast northern expanses as a "zone of sustenance," writes Griffen. They did not think that they or anyone else owned the land, but that it was a territory to be occupied only temporarily and from which they could take food and other supplies they needed. In accordance with the concept of "use rights," Apaches believed that goods and animals belonged to everyone and were there for the taking. Thus raiding was a livelihood, a way of making a living. Since war was a matter of bravery, courage, and strength, it followed that Apache objectives were vengeance and acquisition of resources rather than conquest. Apaches recognized a Supreme Being, or Creator, who was neither benevolent nor punitive, and was therefore not worshipped. They sought to appease the Evil Spirit, who controlled their destinies, but for the most part Apaches lived for the present with little regard for the hereafter. Apache groups spoke the same language, though their accents differed, and each group employed its own local terminology.[11]

Physically the Apaches were endowed with exceptionally robust constitutions. They were quick, nimble, and agile. Extremely gluttonous when food was abundant, they were nevertheless able to withstand great hunger and thirst. For meat, the Apaches stole Spanish horses and cattle, or hunted deer, antelope, bear, pig, panther, and porcupine; but their common food was the prickly pear, yucca, saguaro, acorns, pine nuts, and above all, mescal.[12]

While Apaches were bold, proud, and jealous of their liberty, they were also peevish, inconstant, and distrustful. They usually dwelt in the most rugged and mountainous regions, in natural fortifications where they found abundant water, wood, wild fruits, and game. The men dressed in deer or antelope skins, with a headdress adorned with feathers or horns, and moccasins. The women also dressed in skins fashioned as a blouse and skirt, moccasins, and necklaces of deer and antelope hooves, shell, fish spines, or fragrant roots. The men did the hunting and fighting, armed with lances and bows and arrows. The women cared for the horses, made utensils, cured and tanned hides, carried water and firewood, collected seeds and fruits, made bread, sowed and reaped the crops, accompanied the men on expeditions, and drove the stolen livestock. Each man had as many wives as he could support and gained prestige from the number of huts his family occupied.[13]

The basic unit of Apache social organization was the rancheria, composed of families of kinsmen by blood or marriage. Each rancheria, led by a headman or chief, was independent, and each member of the rancheria was a free agent. After complying with the duties of kinship and etiquette, he made his own decisions and was solely responsible for them. Leadership of the rancheria rested on a man's personal influence. He could use only the power of his personality, but not force, to persuade others to take a particular line of action. It was the warrior's own choice whether to go into battle, and no one was obliged to accept the agreements rancheria leaders concluded with Spaniards or Mexicans. The chief's primary responsibility was for the food, safety, clothes, and well-being of the rancheria members. This fluidity and informality of Apache leadership, it should be emphasized, was difficult for outsiders to understand; and for their part, the Apaches could never understand that a peace agreement made in one place was also binding in another. Each rancheria was a pure and simple autonomous unit.[14]

VICEROY BERNARDO DE GÁLVEZ—HIS INSTRUCCIÓN OF 1786

During the period of the American Revolution the Spanish monarchy again became heavily involved in European international affairs. Regarding the struggle of the American patriots against Great Britain as an unparalleled opportunity to recover Florida, which Spain had lost in 1763, the Spanish monarchy declared war on Great Britain in 1779. Under the effective leadership of Bernardo de Gálvez, governor of Spanish Louisiana, the entire Mississippi River valley was brought under Spanish control. Then followed the defeat of British forces in 1780 at Mobile Bay, and at Pensacola Bay a year later. In the Treaty of Paris of 1783, Spain recovered Florida and retained the Louisiana Territory west of the Mississippi River.[15]

The Interior Provinces in 1784 were placed once more under the Viceroyalty of New Spain. The following year one of the most dynamic and brilliant frontier officials of the century took over the viceregal office: Bernardo de Gálvez, nephew of José de Gálvez, former governor of Spanish Louisiana, and hero of Pensacola Bay. The able and experienced Jacobo Ugarte y Loyola was named commandant general of the Interior Provinces under Viceroy Gálvez's direct authority.[16]

The viceroy, who had mastered Indian psychology during his decade and a half of frontier experience, set forth his new Indian policy in a document known as the *Instrucción* of 1786. While it incorporated much of Spain's traditional Indian policy, it presented several new features. First of all, he pointed out that Spain would wage relentless war on hostile Indians to the point of extermination if necessary; second, Spain would also continue to rely on alliances with those Indian groups who would make war on the hostiles; and third, he suggested that those Indians who sought peace would be settled near the presidios and made dependent on the Spaniards through gifts, supplies, food, alcohol, firearms, and ammunition. The viceroy made it clear, however, that the firearms would be poorly made and soon in need of repair or replacements, all to keep the Indians from using the devastating bow and arrow. This policy, which Gálvez labeled "peace by deceit," governed Spanish-Indian relations on the northern frontier for the remainder of the colonial period. "A bad peace," he remarked, "was better than a good war."[17]

Gálvez's untimely death on 30 November 1786 delayed implementation of his program. His successor in the viceregal office was Manuel Antonio Flores, a strong supporter of the traditional "search-and-destroy" approach. He reorganized the Interior Provinces into two districts, and named to one of them Colonel Juan Ugalde, a hard-liner like himself. Viceroy Flores served for two years, and in 1789 the Conde de Revillagigedo, who supported the Gálvez program, was named viceroy. He united the two districts under the capable and effective Brigadier Pedro de Nava and in 1792 declared the Interior Provinces once again independent of the viceregal office. For more than a decade Nava, an enthusiastic and vigorous supporter of the Gálvez program, brought a large measure of peace and stability to the northern frontier. In the meantime, in 1789 the presidio of San Elizario was moved upriver to its future location on the hacienda of Los Tiburcios.[18]

LOS TIBURCIOS

The roots of the agricultural community of Los Tiburcios reach far to the north and deep into the past of seventeenth-century New Mexico to the modest ranch of Francisco de Ortega and his wife, Isabel de Zamora, in the Sandia district. The paterfamilias was a mulatto *"de color pardo"* from Zacatecas, where he had been born around 1615. Although it is uncertain when he first journeyed to New Mexico, by the mid-1640s Ortega was living there, having attained the rank of sergeant.[19] In 1653 Governor Hernando de Ugarte y la Concha certified Captain Ortega's service record, stating that he had participated in all the most important expeditions that have taken place in the past, both those of punishment and war and those of pacification. He has demonstrated his valor as a very excellent soldier in the wars waged on the enemy.[20]

By around 1650 Francisco had married Isabel, and together they had begun a family. They had at least two known children: Pablo and Tiburcio, the latter born around 1655.[21]

Pablo de Ortega served as alcalde mayor of the Jemez district during the 1670s.[22] Following the 1680 Pueblo Revolt, he fled to Nueva Vizcaya and took up residence in the area around San Juan de la Concepción, Las Cruces, and the Valle de Torreón.[23]

Although we do not know what he thought about his brother's desertion, Tiburcio chose to remain with the colony-in-exile in El Paso. He was listed in 1680 among the survivors as a scribe accompanied by his wife, Margarita de Otón; two children; his mother; siblings; nephews; nieces; and servants.[24]

When Governor Diego de Vargas conducted a census of the area communities from 22 December 1692 to 2 January 1693, Tiburcio de Ortega and his family were living in El Paso. In the twelve years since their arrival as refugees in El Paso, the family had grown. At that time, Tiburcio and Margarita had five children. A daughter, María, was thirteen. Their four boys were Antonio, twelve;

Isidro, eight; Pablo, four; and Gregorio, two. Ortega also had three female Indian dependents, Luisa, Juana, and Anastasia, as well as a male dependent named Felipe.[25]

Beginning with his own offspring, Tiburcio initiated an Ortega family tradition of naming children—males and females—Tiburcio, after himself and the early Christian martyr, St. Tiburtius.[26] Hence his sons, Antonio and Isidro, were also known as Antonio Tiburcio and Isidro Tiburcio. In subsequent generations there would be Ortega males with names such as Diego Tiburcio and females named Antonia or María Josefa Tiburcio de Ortega.[27] In this way, Tiburcio came to be used as though it were a part of a compound surname, Tiburcio de Ortega, and in the usage of the eighteenth century, the place where the extended Tiburcio de Ortega family resided was referred to as Los Tiburcios.[28] The male descendants of Tiburcio de Ortega also continued the tradition of government service that Francisco had begun in New Mexico. Antonio Tiburcio de Ortega served as *teniente de alcalde mayor* in the El Paso district, and his son, Diego Tiburcio de Ortega, was *teniente de justicia mayor* of the lower Rio Grande valley pueblos of Ysleta, Senecú, and Socorro.[29]

In 1724 the *maestre de campo*, Luis Granillo, sold land south of El Paso to Antonio Tiburcio de Ortega, then in his forties. According to the description contained in the documents, the property consisted of

two *sitios de estancia* down the Río del Norte, one of which runs north to south beginning one long league from Socorro Pueblo as far as the old presidio and east to west from said Río del Norte to the hills; the other sitio is farther downriver, forming a bend as far as the place called Estero Largo, bounded on the east by said river and on the west by the hills, for the price and amount of 100 pesos *de oro común.*

Along the west boundary of the northernmost sitio, at the base of the hills, was a well-known landmark called Loma Blanca. On the eastern boundary, on the east side of the river, was a hill that was more prominent than the others.[30]

Because of the lack of precision in the measurements expressed, it is impossible to determine the exact size of the property Antonio Tiburcio de Ortega purchased. The sitio de *estancia de ganado menor* was equal to 3,333⅓ varas or 1,927 acres (780 hectares), while the *estancia de ganado mayor* was the equivalent of 5,000 varas or 4,335 acres (1,755 hectares). That means that the land destined to become the *rancho* of Nuestra Señora de la Soledad de los Tiburcios had either 3,854 or 8,670 acres, which would be around either 6 or 13½ square miles.[31] By way of comparison, the Hacienda de San Antonio, which Governor Antonio de Valverde Cosío established on the east bank of the Rio Grande opposite the Ortega property as early as 1711, consisted of some twelve to sixteen sitios, which made it six to eight times larger than the neighboring farm.[32]

It is unclear when Los Tiburcios went into operation. When the bishop of Durango, Benito Crespo, visited New Mexico in 1730, he made no mention of Los Tiburcios in describing his activities in the El Paso area.[33] El Paso area tithe records from Durango for as late as 1736 do not show Los Tiburcios.[34] Marriage records for the following year, however, indicate that Indian servants of Antonio Tiburcio de Ortega were present in Las Caldas, which was adjacent to the Hacienda de San Antonio and across the river from Los Tiburcios. By 1739 similar sacramental records show that Antonio's rancho was in operation, although a census conducted that year for the governor of New Mexico, Gaspar Domingo de Mendoza, did not list Los Tiburcios as a separate community among the towns in the El Paso area.[35] Fray Miguel de Menchero's 1744 report also failed to note Los Tiburcios. Nevertheless, his accompanying map clearly indicated the "haciendas of Los Tiburcios and San Antonio."[36]

Writing in late 1749 to ecclesiastical authorities in Durango with regard to tithe collection in his jurisdiction, the alcalde mayor of El Paso and presidial captain, Alonso Victores Rubín de Celis, commented on local haciendas. By his reckoning, there had only been three "opulent haciendas" in the district, all of which had fallen on hard times. His hacienda, located upriver from El Paso, had been washed away in a flood. The hacienda that had for-

merly belonged to Governor Valverde Cosío and then his son-in-law, Captain José Valentín de Aganza, could no longer be planted. As for the Hacienda de Carrizal, it was in nearly as bad shape.[37]

Five years later Manuel Antonio San Juan, then captain of the presidio, offered his assessment of the situation of El Paso haciendas. He stated that as recently as 1752, there were still two in operation, Carrizal and Ojo Caliente, both of which had been abandoned by 1754. Of the earlier "abundant and opulent" Hacienda de San Antonio, nothing remained; the Sumas and their allies had destroyed it through their ceaseless raiding. As for Captain Rubín de Celis's property, San Juan did not consider it a hacienda; rather he termed it a *labor*, or farm.[38] Nevertheless, it must have been a large operation, since he deemed it worthy of mention that heavy snows in the interior of the province had led to flooding that caused the Rio Grande to jump its banks, inundating low-lying areas and carrying off the crops sown in Rubín de Celis's fields.[39]

Los Tiburcios may not have begun to flourish until sometime after the mid-1750s, or it may simply never have been considered a true hacienda. A muster in July 1762 of male heads of households available for militia duty recorded 31 citizens and servants, and three years later an anonymous statistical report on New Mexico gave the population of the Hacienda of Los Tiburcios as 210: 21

families of citizens comprising 157 individuals and 10 genízaro families with 44 members. That made Los Tiburcios the smallest of the six communities identified in the census, but one with a substantial population for a largely family agricultural enterprise.[40]

Los Tiburcios, like the other riverine communities in the El Paso area, did not develop in the typical New World fashion, clustered around a rectilinear plaza. When the new lieutenant governor, Antonio María Daroca, arrived in El Paso in 1773, he noted that in all the river communities, which were thickly settled "like the gardens of Murcia," the landowners built their homes in the middle of their property. Thus their houses were not side-by-side, as in a typical Hispanic community.[41] In that sense, they resembled the settlements that characterized the colony upriver in New Mexico in the eighteenth century, which were often nothing more than groups of households forming an extended family.

From the outset, the history of Nuestra Señora de la Soledad cannot be separated from Tiburcio de Ortega's extended-family network. How many of Antonio Tiburcio de Ortega's siblings and their families participated in agricultural activities is unknown. By the 1750s, however, all of his heirs and their families were active at Los Tiburcios. Antonio Tiburcio de Ortega's children were as follows: Diego, Bernardo, Juan, Antonia, and María Josefa Tiburcio de Ortega. Antonia was the wife of Alejo Guerra, and

María Josefa was married to Antonio López. Antonio's brother, Esteban, was also living there.[42] The Durán and Luján families, which were closely related to the Tiburcio de Ortega family, also had many members living at Los Tiburcios at that time.[43]

A detailed listing of tithes for 1779 provides interesting information on agricultural activities at Los Tiburcios. For that year, Los Tiburcios paid no tithes on the following crops grown in the El Paso area: grapes, peas, green beans, wheat, chile, cotton, and garlic. Maize was the only crop for which there was considerable production. Los Tiburcios tithed a total of 67 *almudes* of maize. This placed it second among the communities in the El Paso district in maize production. El Paso tithed 127 almudes, San Lorenzo 64 almudes, Senecú 6 1/2 almudes, Ysleta 3 almudes, and Socorro 21 almudes. Tithes were paid on only two other products from Los Tiburcios, 24 almudes of beans and 10 chickens. Of the eighteen individuals who paid tithes from Los Tiburcios, ten are clearly identifiable as members of the extended Ortega family.[44]

Without putting too much emphasis on a report of a single year's agricultural production as reflected in tithe records, it seems plausible that by 1779 the population of Los Tiburcios was static if not in decline. If the eighteen people who paid tithes that year are taken to represent heads of households, even considering that not every family in Los Tiburcios was involved in agriculture, then it is clear that at most the population was not markedly larger than it had been a decade and a half earlier and may well have been smaller. This situation is partially attributable to disease in the El Paso area, such as the typhus epidemic of 1764, and largely to increased hostility on the part of the Apaches and ill-starred military strategy, which led people to abandon the exposed position that Los Tiburcios occupied.[45]

The removal of the presidio of El Paso to Carrizal in 1773, the year Captain Daroca began his service there, exacerbated the normal difficulty of defending Los Tiburcios, some twenty miles south of El Paso. In its place, Daroca attempted to organize militia units. Los Tiburcios was required to contribute men-at-arms to form, with men from Socorro, one of six companies for the El Paso area, but the ranks were slow to fill. The local militia proved unable to contain the Apaches. In 1774 the presidio of Guajoquilla, which had been located near present-day Jiménez, Chihuahua, since 1753, was moved to the valley of San Elceario, just under forty miles downriver from Los Tiburcios. This move, however, also failed to provide adequate protection.[46]

Still, it is difficult to pinpoint the beginning of the end of Los Tiburcios. Whether the dramatic population decline had begun as early as 1779, by 1784 the number of residents of Los Tiburcios had dwindled. In the census taken that year, the citizens of Los Tiburcios were included with those of Socorro. A comparison of another census taken three years later permits identification of many of the citizens of Los Tiburcios. The latter census, taken on 9 May 1787, listed only fifty-five individuals, almost all closely related to the Ortega family. In fewer than twenty-five years, the apparently once-thriving community had suffered an almost 75 percent drop in population.[47]

Depopulation and incessant Apache attacks came together with high-level military strategy in the spring of 1787, leading to the abandonment of Los Tiburcios. In late April, Colonel José Antonio Rengel proposed to Commandant General Jacobo de Ugarte y Loyola that Los Tiburcios was well suited to locate Apaches in a peace camp. Ugarte responded that he was very much in agreement that Los Tiburcios was the best location for settling the Mescaleros.[48] By 14 May, less than a week after the census, the correspondence between Rengel and Ugarte referred to Los Tiburcios as having been abandoned.[49]

The order to leave Los Tiburcios has not surfaced, although many of the details surrounding its issuance have survived. According to testimony of Domingo de Ortega, the son of Diego Tiburcio de Ortega and self-styled "owner" of Los Tiburcios, frequent deaths and thefts resulting from Apache depredations led to an order from "on high" to abandon Los Tiburcios. The military authorities had determined that the enemy was too much for its inhabitants, even when the militia and citizenry from

El Paso lent a hand. After receiving the order, Ortega traveled to Chihuahua to meet with Ugarte y Loyola.[50]

As Ortega recalled their encounter, Ugarte y Loyola listened to every detail with great understanding. To provide a solution to the difficult situation, the commandant general decided to transfer the presidio of San Elizario to Los Tiburcios. There Ortega placed himself at the disposal of Francisco Martínez, who was commissioned to improve the site for the construction of the presidio. Ortega further stated that he voluntarily ceded to the king of Spain land south of the site where the presidio was eventually located, as far as Las Arenas, a distance of approximately one and a half leagues. All that remained within his boundaries in that direction, as well as everything to the north, he reserved for his fields and for his heirs.[51]

Ortega's visit may have exerted the influence over Ugarte y Loyola's decision that the old man claimed, and his offer to give land to the crown may have been welcome. Given that the order to abandon Los Tiburcios preceded their meeting in Chihuahua, however, it seems just as likely that plans to relocate the presidio of San Elizario upriver to Los Tiburcios had already been formulated and that Ortega's generosity was irrelevant, from the standpoint of military planning. Whatever the case, by mid-May 1787, Los Tiburcios had been abandoned and by mid-August 1788, the decision to relocate the presidio of San Elizario had been reached.[52]

CONSTRUCTION OF THE PRESIDIO OF SAN ELIZARIO

On 17 August 1788, Francisco Javier de Uranga, lieutenant governor of El Paso, wrote area pueblos requesting laborers to work on the presidio of San Elizario when it was relocated to Los Tiburcios. The citizens and adults of Ysleta agreed to provide twelve days' work each, and those of Senecú made a similar commitment for two weeks.[53] Another six months passed before the inspector and captain, Diego de Borica, informed Uranga that on 14 February 1789 he was ordering Lieutenant Colonel Francisco Martínez and Captain Juan Antonio de Arce to Los Tiburcios to select the new location for the presidio of San Elizario. Land in Los Tiburcios was to be marked off so that a presidio modeled on the one at Carrizal could be constructed.[54] Adobes were to be made before the rains came, wood was to be cut, and walls were to be built. Had these instructions been followed to the letter, the resulting presidio of San Elizario would have been an adobe structure built on a more or less rectangular plan and completely enclosed with one or two diamond-shaped bastions, which were rather like ample towers. Inside the fortified perimeter, measuring approximately 200 varas by 100 varas, would have been living quarters for officers and men; a *plaza de armas*, or parade ground; various work- and storerooms; a chapel; and pens for livestock. This would have been much how Carrizal appeared.[55]

Based on a plan of the Mexican presidio drawn in 1847, it can be seen that certain modifications were made in San Elizario that deviated from the Carrizal model and in some respects from most other frontier presidios. Most notable is the fact that there were two rectilinear walls, one completely enclosing the other, an unusual design for a presidio.[56] The description cited by Roscoe and Margaret Conkling indicates that the presidio's outside wall en-closed some twelve hundred square feet. The inner wall en-closed the officers' quarters, barracks, the chapel, a magazine, and other buildings. Stables were located between the two walls. Two towers were on the inner wall, and both walls were of adobe construction and more than four feet thick and around eighteen feet high. All the buildings were of adobe.[57]

While this description may reflect some exaggeration, particularly with respect to the height of the walls, it is roughly in line with that of other late eighteenth-century frontier presidios. Based on archaeological evidence gathered at other presidio sites, the perimeter wall of a presidio could be more than three feet thick.[58] Given that no mention is made of a second wall in the extant documents that relate to the construction of the presidio at San Elizario, and its obvious deviation from Spanish military design at the time of the presidio's construction, it seems plausible that the outer wall was a later addition. Its prin-cipal purpose, as noted above, seems to have been to enclose livestock, presumably in times of danger. The interior wall was probably considered the perimeter wall of the presidio proper. A contemporary presidio in Tucson had a perimeter wall more than two feet thick and twelve feet high.[59] The presidio of San Elizario was also larger and more nearly square than Carrizal, measuring some 215 by 210 varas.[60] Finally, there were two defensive towers at San Elizario, both rectangular rather than diamond-shaped. One was located at a corner of the wall, characteristic of presidios constructed after the *Reglamento* of 1772.[61]

The move upriver to Los Tiburcios from the original site of the presidio of San Elizario near present-day El Porvenir, Chihuahua, must have followed Borica's directive to relocate in short order. By late April, Indians from Socorro delivered 1,500 adobes for use in construction of the presidio.[62] By early June, Commandant General Jacobo Ugarte y Loyola was praising the outstanding progress being made on the presidio and offering some suggestions. Ugarte y Loyola reminded the man commissioned to supervise the building of the presidio of San Elizario, Francisco Martínez, to take care that the walls were thick enough, that double layers of straw wall covering were used if the ridge-pieces were not yet in place, and that every care should be taken to protect the adobes that had been made against damage by the coming rains.[63]

Martínez, already the chief military man with respect

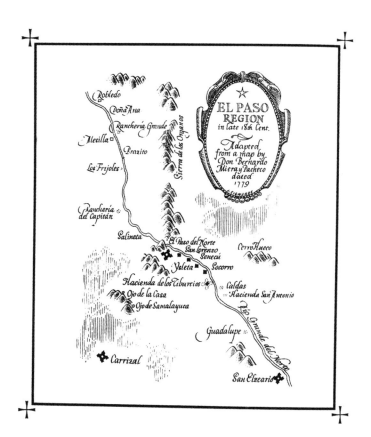

to the site of the presidio, was also given civil authority to oversee the proper location of the proposed pueblo and the distribution of house lots and land. Neither the captain of San Elizario nor the captain of the militia of El Paso was permitted direct communication with troops outside the district while the commission lasted.

At present, it is uncertain how the planned pueblo related physically to the presidio compound. Clearly it was to be protected by another wall. Rather than the 1,000-vara wall that Lieutenant Colonel Martínez suggested, the commandant general thought that 600 varas would suffice to protect the pueblo. The streets of the pueblo were to be wide and straight from north to south, oriented for the best ventilation. The house lots did not have to include gardens, but corrals and other conveniences should be provided according to the skills of each individual.

Land for gardens was to be allotted first from within the 600 varas in small plots, keeping some in reserve for future inhabitants. Beyond the gardens, Martínez was to provide land for farming and explain the distribution of land to the captain of San Elizario. Everyone was to receive an inventory of the land distribution, which would serve as a title, and copies were to be recorded in a book to remain in the presidial archive. The captain of San Elizario and the captain of the militia of El Paso were expressly forbidden to impede anyone who wished to move to take advantage of this offer. As soon as such an individual arrived at Martínez's jurisdiction, he or she became subject to his authority alone.

Work on the new presidio and pueblo was in full swing during the summer months of 1790; crews of twenty-five to thirty men labored on the site.[64] At the time of the first inspection of the new presidio that May, no specific mention was made of the status of construction. The inspector, Lieutenant Colonel Antonio Cordero, did note, however, that Alferez Antonio de Arce, whom he described as spirited and well suited for work because of his education and robust health, held a commission for the construction of the presidio. This was in addition to his regular duties as a paymaster, for which he was known for keeping good records.[65]

The commandant of San Elizario received word in the winter of 1791 that he was to employ prisoners sent from El Paso on construction at the presidio.[66] In January 1793 Commandant General Pedro de Nava ordered him to press ahead on the work of the presidio, especially the task of roofing the lodging for the paymaster of the company. He also ordered Uranga to encourage the citizens to send the peons who were required to work on the presidio and use their oxen to take wood and old barrels from the abandoned site of the San Elizario presidio to the new one. The wood was to be used for building houses.[67]

In February 1793 Nava appointed Manuel Vidal de Lorca, a captain from the presidio of San Carlos, as commandant of San Elizario.[68] He instructed him to complete the work on the presidio. Vidal de Lorca informed Lieutenant Governor Uranga that he expected to be sent twenty laborers from Socorro. He asked for a list of everyone who had promised to contribute work on the presidio and failed to do so.[69] Vidal de Lorca repeated his request in March, citing the need for twenty men from Socorro to work on the presidio in order to fulfill their commitment of 130 days' work. Those citizens from El Paso who promised to work were also called to San Elizario, along with a dozen Indians from one of the pueblos. Master mason Antonio Cordero,[70] who had already been paid for forty-seven days at the rate of a peso a day, was ordered to report for work.[71] Vidal de Lorca employed an enlarged workforce of fifty men through the month of April, when he anticipated keeping them on for another, unspecified period at the usual rate of three *reales* a day.[72]

On 1 August 1793, Commandant General Nava prepared a detailed plan for reforming the militia of El Paso and dispatched it to the minister of war in Spain, the Conde del Campo de Alange. Nava judged the militia unnecessary, given the decline in Indian raiding and the presence of the presidio of San Elizario nearby. He noted that since 12 October 1778, some 4,556 pesos 2 reales had accumulated to support militia activity. The money came from holding in reserve 2 percent of the *alcabala*, or sales tax, that the citizens of El Paso paid. The commandant general proposed applying this money, which was already on deposit, toward the completion of the presidio of San Elizario.

When Viceroy Manuel Antonio Flores ordered the relocation of the presidio of San Elizario to Los Tiburcios, he had directed Mariscal de Campo Ugarte y Loyola to carry out the move without cost to the royal treasury. Nava reported that the donations the troops made were insufficient to provide transportation of building materials that the citizens of El Paso offered to furnish, as were the efforts of the peons and the assistance of local carters. As a result the presidio had not been completed. In order to prevent the ruin of what had been built and finish construction, Nava had felt compelled to take 2,000 pesos from the Fondo de Gratificación. By his own admission, the commandant general classified the situation as urgent. Because he thought that the minister of the treasury, Diego de Gardoqui, might see fit to intervene in the matter of the alcabala, Nava sent him a copy of the proposal he had made to the conde del Campo de Alange.[73] The response to Nava's proposal is unknown. What is clear is that construction continued on the presidio of San Elizario. By early December Vidal de Lorca requested additional wood from the lieutenant governor; he was almost out of the one thousand vigas the citizens of El Paso had brought him.

Vidal de Lorca's death at Apache hands in March 1794 was a blow to the presidio,[74] robbing it of an able commandant, but it did not halt construction. In fact, the last specific mention of building at the presidio did not come until the end of that year, and it implied that work would be continuing for some time to come. Writing in December 1794, Commandant General Nava informed the lieutenant governor of El Paso that he had sentenced a soldier convicted of murdering an Indian to two years' hard labor on the construction of the presidio of San Elizario.[75]

The ongoing need for frequent repairs at San Elizario was shown at the end of the Mexican period when the days of the presidio were nearly over. On 5 June 1841, the *juez de primera instancia* of El Paso, Joaquín Velarde, remanded two prisoners to the custody of the commandant of the presidio of San Elizario. As punishment for their crimes, they were to work on the reconstruction of the presidio. Again on 17 June 1841, the juez de primera instancia sent three more prisoners to the commandant of the presidio of San Elizario. The magistrate specified that they were to work on repairing the wall of the presidio.[76]

In some senses, work on the presidio was never ending. With an extensive compound surrounded by massive walls—all of adobe—frequent seasonal repair would have been an ongoing activity. A growing pueblo also meant that construction probably rarely ceased in the early years of the life of the presidio of San Elizario in its new location at Los Tiburcios, and at least routine maintenance probably continued until the presidio was abandoned.

THE PRESIDIO OF
SAN ELIZARIO, 1789–1821

THE RELOCATION OF THE PRESIDIO TO SAN ELIZARIO

THE RELOCATION OF THE PRESIDIO OF SAN ELIZARIO

The new Indian policy promulgated by Viceroy Gálvez in 1786, the 216-paragraph *Instrucción*, was what one historian has called a "combination of the mailed fist and the olive branch."[1] Indians were offered the choice between all-out warfare and peace on the Spaniards' terms. The linchpin of the program was the concept referred to as *Indios de paz*, loosely translated as Indians at peace. The tenets of the new canon required that the effort to convert the Indians, especially the Apaches, should be set aside for a time. They should be urged to settle near presidios, where they would be given food, liquor, tobacco, and old or poor quality firearms. The objective of this program was to make the Apaches dependent on the Spaniards for their survival.[2]

The definite opinions of the commandant inspector of Nueva Vizcaya and New Mexico, Colonel José Antonio Rengel, about where to settle Apaches at peace had a direct impact on the future of the presidio then located in the valley of San Elceario. Rengel thought that the presidio of El Norte was unsuitable for the establishment of Mescalero rancherias.[3] Ill-equipped to provide provisions for such a large group of Indians because it lacked sufficient good farm land, El Norte was also too near the expanding Comanche territory. Los Tiburcios, by contrast, had ample supplies of everything needed to settle the Apaches in a successful peace camp.[4] The land was cleared and fertile and, given the nearby communities, the site was perfect for the trade fairs where hides were exchanged. Ugarte informed Rengel that they were very much in agreement on the choice of Los Tiburcios as the best location for settling the Mescaleros.[5]

The once-thriving ranching community had suffered an almost 75 percent decline in population in less than twenty-five years for reasons that will be detailed below. This explains why in 1787 Rengel referred to the abandoned pueblo of Los Tiburcios as a possible site for relocating the Mescalero Apaches. It also suggests that its suitability as a potential resettlement site played an important role in moving the presidio upriver. Hence the improved defense of the El Paso area was not the only consideration affecting the decision to relocate the presidio of San Elizario.[6]

Two Mescalero leaders who traveled to El Paso to parley with Rengel expressed their reservations about his plan. They cited their preference for hunting rather than farming and living in separate camps as opposed to congregating under a single leader. The Mescaleros also thought that the presidio of El Norte afforded more security than did Los Tiburcios.[7]

While the matter awaited resolution, the commandant inspector issued orders regulating the dealings between citizens and Indians at peace in the El Paso area. The *justicias* of the Lower Valley pueblos were directed to see that while the Indians at peace were across the river, no one should go to meet or trade with them. When they were on the El Paso side of the river in the pueblos, trade was to be conducted in the public plazas and only after notifying the authorities.[8]

BEGINNINGS OF THE APACHE PEACE PROGRAM

The decision to relocate the presidio of San Elizario to Los Tiburcios had been made by mid-August 1788.[9] After it was moved early in the following year, the presidio and Apache peace establishments grew together. The full company complement in the first year at the new location included a captain, often called commandant; a lieutenant; two alfereces; a chaplain; an armorer; a drummer; and sixty-six other soldiers, including two sergeants, two corporals, and four riflemen.[10] In February 1790 three Mescalero Apache leaders, whom the Spaniards called *capitancillos*, or little captains, sought peace in El Paso: Volante; Alegre; and Bigotes, El Bermejo.[11] Lieutenant Governor Francisco Javier de Uranga received the Indians' emissary, Bigotes's son, in his home and fed him. He also

gave him a peso's worth of cigarettes, four reales' worth of candy, and a large knife.[12] Ugarte y Loyola informed Lieutenant Governor Uranga that they should travel to Chihuahua to discuss a lasting peace with the commandant general. He also ordered the captain of the El Paso militia and the commandant of San Elizario to provide an escort should the Indians leave from either place. As for the expenses of the Indian emissary, Uranga was to apply to the captain of the El Paso militia for those and similar costs.[13]

During the following month, more Apaches asked for peace in El Paso. Ugarte y Loyola acknowledged receipt of a report from Uranga concerning the return of a Mescalero emissary and the arrival and return of a Gila to one of his rancherias. Ugarte y Loyola advised Uranga not to express his satisfaction at requests for peace. He should have the Mescalero capitancillos, Alegre and Volante, take Domingo Díaz with them if they were going straight from El Paso to Chihuahua. The commandant general, whose mistrust of the Gila Apaches did not extend to the Mescaleros, urged Uranga to exercise caution with the Gilas, particularly since they had sought peace in El Paso before without formalizing the arrangement. Finally, Ugarte y Loyola directed Uranga to solicit from any Indian requesting peace the following information: what rancheria was he from, where it was located, who its capitancillo was, how many people it contained, whether all were in agree-

ment, and what the motive for seeking peace was.[14]

In June 1790 the Apache leader who was to figure most prominently at San Elizario presidio sued for peace. Spaniards knew him as Pedro Barrio, or more commonly as Capitancillo Barrio; to his people he was Nzaze. Barrio came with a few warriors and Capitancillo Arco from the Sacramento Mountains. Because Ugarte y Loyola was eager to come to terms with them, he permitted Uranga to set peace conditions should the Apache leaders prove reluctant to travel to Chihuahua.[15]

Ugarte y Loyola would allow Capitancillo Barrio to settle in peace in El Paso, if he wished to live as the Chiricahuas did at Bacoachic in Sonora. The Lipiyan leader, Capitancillo El Calvo, could settle at the El Norte presidio as Alegre, Volante, José, and Montera Blanca had. Still, the Indians were to travel to Chihuahua to discuss peace with Ugarte y Loyola. To assist Uranga, Ugarte y Loyola ordered the commandant of San Elizario to send him an Apache interpreter if one were available.[16] Subsequent testimony indicated that the Mescalero leaders settled at the presidio of El Norte, although El Calvo and his people continued to live free.[17]

Barrio, however, must have found the terms to his liking. In June 1790 two warriors swam the swollen Rio Grande with word that when the high water subsided, Capitancillos Barrio and Arco would come to El Paso. Eighteen Indian men and two women from their rancherias came in.[18] The following month he and two other Apaches from the Sierra Blancas, twelve warriors, and five women requested peace in El Paso. Another sixty Apaches and their families awaited the outcome of their petition on the other side of the river. Once again Ugarte y Loyola ordered Uranga to have the capitancillos travel to Chihuahua to discuss the matter with him.[19]

Despite his seeming acquiescence, Capitancillo Barrio proved to be a particular irritant to the presidio of San Elizario, for he and his numerous followers were reluctant to settle among the other Apaches at peace and Spaniards. While they preferred the other side of the Rio Grande, opposite El Paso, the military authorities were adamant that Barrio and his people should live next to San Elizario. The Spaniards considered him recalcitrant, untrustworthy, and a proven thief. Because other Apache leaders were cause for far greater concern, on occasion Barrio was lauded for his exemplary behavior and offered up as a model for other Apache leaders.[20]

When Ugarte y Loyola left his post in August to attend to urgent business, he notified Uranga that all military and Indian matters should be referred to either his successor, Brigadier Pedro de Nava, or Lieutenant Colonel Antonio Cordero.[21] Cordero's assistance was invoked almost immediately, for that same month, the enemy attacked and raided Senecú. In response, Cordero told Uranga to advise Barrio that true peace required him to warn the Spaniards of impending hostilities. Other Indians at peace did so and further offered to pursue the offending parties even if they were their relatives.[22] Cordero also ordered Uranga to prepare for a sixty-day campaign by 15 October. When word arrived from Captain Juan Antonio de Arce, who was to pay for the supplies, forty citizens and Indians were to be ready to leave.[23]

Cordero's vigilance must have seemed particularly opportune, for in early October he received an alarming report from Uranga: All the Apaches at peace established in El Paso had been absent for the entire month of September. Whatever fears this may have initially aroused, however, were put to rest over time, as it became evident that the Indians were leaving and returning to the settlement as a matter of course.[24]

The winter of 1790 was calm, and as the new year began, Uranga was able to note that the Apaches in the Organ Mountains continued at peace. Cordero directed him to foster this friendship and try to get them to induce the Sacramento Mountain Apaches to join this alliance. Although the peace seemed to be holding, Cordero thought it appropriate to forward a communication from Blas de Aramburu, commandant of the presidio of El Príncipe, cautioning against trusting the Mescalero Apaches.[25]

Good news about Uranga's progress in making peace

with the Faraón Apaches prompted further directives from Cordero in early February. While he agreed that Barrio's complaint against Quenlca and Tlayaleel was justified, since they were at peace with the Spaniards, they should not be apprehended. Barrio himself would have to undertake whatever vengeance he sought. In any event, the Capitán Grande would be available in El Paso at month's end should the capitancillo wish to visit him. With regard to the Indians in the Robledo Mountains, Uranga was to continue his efforts to make peace and at the same time repeat his request for them to return a kidnapped boy and horses they had stolen. If they refused to come to terms, Uranga was to select some Indian allies to guide the troops against them.

Cordero further ordered Uranga to ascertain why El Calvo had taken his rancheria to New Mexico and then inform the governor of the cause. The lieutenant colonel was somewhat ambivalent about the Indians' insistence on horse-trading, which he thought only encouraged them to steal more horses. While he agreed that it could continue in the interests of humoring them, he was firm that they should trade only their own horses and not those they had stolen.[26]

Uranga's success with the Faraones, while welcome, was not rapid enough for Cordero, who would not allow Apache hostilities in his jurisdiction to go unpunished. Only a week after congratulating the lieutenant governor of El Paso, Cordero ordered Lieutenant Juan Francisco Granados to begin a campaign in the Robledo Mountains against the Faraones who were disturbing the peace established with the Apaches from the Organ and Sacramento Mountains. He was to send 100 men from his 140-man detachment to El Paso to pick up Apache auxiliaries; Uranga, for his part, was also to assist him with several more. He further instructed Uranga to show the commanding officer where the Apaches at peace were living so that he would not mistakenly harm them.[27]

Cordero gave Barrio and his people his assurance that they were still welcome as visitors. He ordered the captain of the San Elizario presidio to loan Uranga horses to transport them. Uranga was to ensure that only a few principal Indians traveled to Chihuahua and was to await Lieutenant Granados's return before their departure.[28]

While Uranga had to pursue some of the Faraón Apaches on the field of battle, others settled in the El Paso area responded favorably to his overtures. By early March Cordero acknowledged his satisfaction with Uranga's report on the peace reigning among the Faraones established at the pueblos in the El Paso jurisdiction and the news that El Calvo had made peace in New Mexico.[29]

In the spring of 1791 Cordero tried to bring more order to the often bewildering situation regarding the various Apache groups. He found the Spanish practice of giving names to the Apaches caused confusion for both parties and ordered that thenceforth Spaniards were to employ the names Apaches used among themselves. Despite this order and an increase in attempts (frequently tortured) to render Apache names into Castilian, the traditional use of epithets continued.[30]

The need for clarification was evident. Because it was difficult to determine whether Apaches at peace or enemy Apaches were responsible for the frequent livestock thefts in the area, it was hard to know which specific ones should be punished. Usually only an officer on the local scene could sort matters for his superiors. Such was the case when Uranga found it necessary to explain to Cordero that, despite what he had heard, Capitancillo Mayá was away and that other Indians had carried out a recent theft of oxen in El Paso.[31]

The presence of unfriendly Apaches in close proximity to those who had accepted peace in the El Paso jurisdiction further confounded the Spaniards and kept circumstances fluid and unsettled. Just as one group would accept peace, another would violate it. This resulted in almost constant campaigning, but always with precautions to avoid disrupting and upsetting the Indians established in peace camps.

In April 1791 Uranga received word from the governor of New Mexico, Fernando de la Concha, that Apaches from the Robledo Mountains were causing problems among the Apaches at peace. The governor went on to add that if Capitancillo El Calvo requested peace, he would grant it, implying that he had either not accepted the terms offered him the previous year or had already broken that peace.[32]

Despite pressures from the Apaches at Robledo, the Faraones at peace in El Paso continued to show signs of their good faith. For that reason Cordero decided to receive their leaders in Chihuahua and ordered the commandant of San Elizario to provide a ten-man escort for those who wanted to meet him.[33] While Cordero was issuing that order, Uranga was departing El Paso with Barrio and two other Apache leaders for Chihuahua, leaving Francisco Javier Bernal in charge. A squadron leader and twelve men from San Elizario formed the escort.[34] Despite Uranga's skillful handling of several Apache groups, a simmering problem remained when he departed. Apaches from the rancheria led by Iticha, known to the Spaniards as Capitancillo Arrieta, were angry because soldiers had killed an Indian who was trying to steal a horse. As yet unaware of this latest problem, and pleased with the example Barrio and the Faraones had set, Cordero still requested information on Indians who were reluctant to make peace.[35]

Among the latter were the rancherias under the leadership of Squielnocten and Bucanneti. Because they were also suspected of livestock thefts, Cordero ordered a force from the presidio of El Norte to seek them out in early

May 1791. Mescaleros were to accompany the troops and the Apaches at peace to advise of the troop movements.[36]

PEDRO DE NAVA'S ADMINISTRATION OF THE APACHE PEACE PROGRAM

Commandant General Nava began instituting piecemeal policy changes in the summer of 1791. Some, like the monthly requirement to send to headquarters the names of the capitancillos and an estimate of the number of Indians at peace, were relatively minor, but provided a useful way to measure how the program was working.[37] Uranga's reports, dutifully filed, sometimes painted a picture that seemed idyllic.

> The Apaches have not given us any trouble in this jurisdiction in all the month of June. The Apaches at peace come and go happily to eat, returning to their rancherias on the other side of the river in the afternoon.

This led Nava to hope that good faith and timely assistance would persuade the Indians to live in the peace camps.[38] On other occasions, Uranga provided valuable details on how fluidly the program worked in practice. Between September and October of 1792, for instance, he recorded a familiar pattern in the movement of Indians into and out of the area. Tlayaleel, who was in El Paso with twenty-five warriors, thirty women, and sixty children in September, left a few of them behind when he went deer hunting in the Ojito de Samalayuca in October. Barrio, Maselchide, and Chineslán were in the Sacramento Mountains during September, while Mayá could be found in the Jornada del Muerto. The following month, the first three were still in the Sacramentos, but nothing had been heard from Mayá.[39]

Other changes were more substantive. In August 1791 Cordero let it be known that when new Apaches requested peace in the future, they would have to surrender their captives.[40] Furthermore, commanders of outposts where there were Apaches at peace would have to rid them of the notion of coming to visit Nava.[41] Although this was a routine practice of long standing, it had resulted in unnecessary expense. Only the most serious matters could justify a trip, and then, only by the smallest number possible. These same Indians were also to be notified that from then on, they would have no right to recover prisoners the Spaniards captured on campaign.[42] The return of relatives was to be considered a favor from the commandant general. Finally came the prohibition on livestock trading with the Apaches at peace in El Paso; thenceforth only unbranded animals could be bought or traded.[43]

Nava shrewdly understood that, aside from a demonstration of his good faith, the return of captive family members was a way to make the Apaches at peace beholden to him. It was a particularly valuable tool, given the frequency with which some family members accepted peace, while others lived among the enemy. Its usefulness was shown when Manuel Rengel ordered the return of the daughter of Tunanita, a venerable Apache leader, after her capture by Spanish troops. Tunanita, a valued ally who had led troops to the rancheria of Vindaviyaya, could scarcely have failed to feel grateful.[44]

Consistent with these policy changes, the Spaniards occasionally returned livestock to Apache leaders. When the Chiricahua leader, Jasquenelté,[45] known to the Spaniards as Capitancillo Ronco,[46] complained that a pair of Apaches at peace had stolen four of his horses, Nava ordered him compensated with replacements. He was to be informed, however, that Capitancillo Cadisóns was saying that Jasquenelté and his people were the cause of the problem.[47]

As the months of Nava's administration passed and his refinements in the program were implemented, Spaniard and Apache developed a modus vivendi. Although the daily activity of the Apaches at peace program in San Elizario cannot be reconstructed from what financial records remain, a sample report from the summer of 1791 gives an idea of how the two groups interacted.

> The alferez and paymaster, Antonio de Arce, and the captain of the presidio of San Elizario, Juan Antonio de Arce, rendered the following account for expenses for the Apaches at peace at from 1 April to 26 June 1791:
>
> 9 April: To two Apaches who came to El Paso from Carrizal, 1 almud of maize and 1 of beans, 2 reales 6 granos
>
> 4 May: To two Apaches who came from El Paso, 2 piloncillos and 2 boxes of cigarettes, 2 reales 4 granos
>
> 12 May: For 1 bull given to the Apaches who came with Lieutenant Ventura Montes from El Norte to El Paso, 11 pesos
>
> 14 May: 1 sheep to the same Apaches, 1 peso 5 reales
>
> 9 June: To Capitancillo Ronco and one Apache who came with him, 2 piloncillos and 4 boxes of cigarettes, 4 reales 8 granos
>
> 14 June: To two Apaches who were here with their families, 1 sheep, 1 peso 5 reales; 2 almudes of maize, 1 of beans, and 4 boxes of cigarettes, 1 peso 3 granos
>
> 17 June: To the same Apaches because they said they were leaving for Carrizal, 2 almudes of maize, 2 piloncillos, and 2 boxes of cigarettes, 7 pesos
>
> Total: 17 pesos 3 reales 9 granos[48]

The following month, Captain Diego de Borica sent twenty bulls for the Apaches at peace and ordered a further twenty-five to be sent. That fall Nava ordered the paymaster of San Elizario, Antonio de Arce, to purchase two hundred fanegas of corn, thirty of beans, and twenty of wheat to have on hand for the Apaches at peace.[49]

In October 1791 Nava delivered a revised set of comprehensive instructions governing the administration of the Indians at peace program. The *Instrucción* ran to thirty-seven articles and in some respects marked a fundamental departure from Gálvez's previous one.[50] Gone was the emphasis on forcing the Indians to accept peace; in its place was the subtler approach of enticing them through gifts, military assistance, and the freedom to pursue traditional activities, such as seasonal hunting. Gálvez's emphasis on trade was replaced by a commitment to provision the Indians modestly at government expense. Gálvez's policies, had they been successful, would have led to the Apaches' wrenching loss of their accustomed lifeways. Nava, by contrast, sought to transform them gradually into useful subjects while allowing them to preserve, at least for a time, their character as a hunting and gathering people.[51]

Nava clearly valued honest dealings with the Indians where Gálvez relied more on cynical duplicity, but it would be wrong to conclude that his *Instrucción* ushered in a benevolent regime. This was particularly so, given his view that Apaches were untrustworthy and wicked. Indians, it should be remembered, were being urged to give up their old way of life, inform on each other, and become agriculturalists. They were also being encouraged to fight against fellow Apaches who had not sued for peace, even if they were relatives.[52]

Crossing Nava's *Instrucción* in the mail were reports that at least seven capitancillos had left the El Paso area.[53] When he learned of this, Nava advised that the Apaches at peace were to be persuaded to leave their families under the Spaniards' protection when they went hunting and gathering, but that they were not to be forced to do so. His new rules were to be adapted to the situation.[54] The Apaches had not broken the peace; Barrio and the others had simply gone out onto the plains to hunt buffalo. When they returned, they were to be treated in accord with Nava's regulations, as was Capitancillo Tlayaleel, who had just offered to make peace and set up his ranchería on the opposite side of the river.[55]

Early in 1792 Nava faced circumstances that led him to make yet another policy change. Since time out of mind, the colonists in area communities had taken Indian children into their homes to raise and employ as domestic servants. Some Indians at peace brought to his attention the case of an Indian girl who had fled the home where she had been deposited to be raised; Capitancillo Barrio had later found her in the Hueco Mountains. Nava ordered that if she was old enough to flee again, she was to be sent to Chihuahua.[56] In a similar instance, Nava clashed with Uranga over the matter of returning a baptized Apache boy to his mother. Nava did not approve of the decision to send the lad back to his mother, but took steps to put a end to the practice of placing Indian children in Spanish homes. He ordered that citizens were no longer to accept Apache children in trade for animals or goods as they had done in the past.[57]

There were some problems that even the *Instrucción* could not resolve. One was the particular susceptibility

Apaches living near Spaniards seemed to have to contagious diseases of European origin. With the catastrophic consequences of the epidemics that had struck the El Paso area still within living memory, it cannot have come as any surprise that those groups affected completely abandoned their peace camps in late March or early April 1792. At the same time, Nava received word in Chihuahua that an unnamed illness had descended on the Apaches in the Sacramento Mountains, killing Capitancillo Azquieyunancha, his wife, and eight warriors. All the other Apache leaders sought refuge in the Guadalupe and Organ Mountains or in the Sierra Blancas [58]

Another was the issue of illegal weapons transactions with the Apaches. In May Nava ordered Cordero to conduct an investigation at the presidio of El Norte and in El Paso about the alleged sale of guns and ammunition to Indians. He was especially concerned about rumors that the Lipiyan Apache leader, Picax Andé Ynstincle de Ugalde, known as El Calvo, and his people were trading horses and mules for munitions. Francisco Javier Bernal testified, however, that he knew of no such activity in El Paso. While it was true that Barrio and Mayá frequented the area, staying mostly in the Sacramento Mountains, El Calvo had never been seen there. Juan Pedro Rivera confirmed the absence of both illegal trading and El Calvo, but noted that Nzaze (Barrio), Maselchide, Tlayaleel, Tuchonchujato (Mayá), and Chineslán had sought peace

there.[59]

Livestock thievery also appeared intractable. Increasing occurrences that spring were blamed principally on those Apaches at peace who had remained. When Nava received a report of minor Apache thefts, he directed Uranga to have the capitancillos of the rancherias where the thieves lived punish them. Similarly when he learned that Barrio had returned several animals, and brought back four stolen horses on another occasion, he praised the capitancillo's behavior and asked the lieutenant governor of El Paso to pass along his appreciation. Barrio was to be held up as an example for the other Apache leaders.[60]

The larceny continued, however, as evidenced by the report that the enemy had carried off another dozen horses and seven head of cattle near El Paso. In response, Nava ordered Uranga to persuade the most reliable Apaches at peace to join a campaign mounted with citizens, militia, and troops from San Elizario, a move consistent with the policy of encouraging the Apaches to fight one another. Nava also instructed Uranga to locate the rancherias headed by Chineslán and Maselchide, since word had it that they were preparing to break the peace.[61] When Nava learned that some Apaches living off the Apaches at peace had carried out another raid on El Paso on 19 July, he dispatched an order for the commandant of San Elizario presidio to send twenty men to reinforce the troops from El Paso.[62]

This last incident underscored a recurrent problem that also resisted solution. It was obvious by the summer of 1792 that groups of Apaches who had refused to settle alongside the presidios were happy to live off the supplies provided to the peaceful Indians.[63] Since this served to support the livestock thefts, which never stopped completely but only seemed to accelerate, the result was a hasty response on the part of the local citizenry. When troops from San Elizario followed up with a punitive raid, as they often did, few animals were recovered; most engagements were inconclusive. The enemy usually disappeared into the mountains or vanished into the desert.

The late summer witnessed a brief respite in hostilities. Despite reports of sporadic attacks in the El Paso jurisdiction, Capitancillo Barrio was living there with his family and those who had joined them. Tunanita and Mayá had located their campsites there as well.[64] The calm was shattered by year's end, however, when twenty warriors under the command of Tujachita descended from the Sierra del Muerto on the El Paso district. Although they sued for peace during the first week of December, this incident indicated how tenuous Spanish control was over the recalcitrant Apaches.[65]

Early in 1793 Nava instituted a fundamental change in the Apaches at peace program, making San Elizario the only gathering point. Captain Manuel Vidal de Lorca, newly assigned to San Elizario from the San Carlos presidio, would be responsible for their administration and oversee the distribution of their customary rations of meat, maize, beans, and cigarettes. All Apaches at peace would now have to report to the presidio, where they would receive identification papers stating the bearer's name, place of origin, destination, and number of days of travel. Spaniards and local Indians were prohibited from admitting any Apache into their homes without these documents.[66]

If Nava hoped by these means to keep a tighter rein on the peaceful Apaches, and perhaps indirectly on the Apaches still at war, his disappointment must have been keen. In the years that followed, hostilities of all sorts, from raids to cattle thefts, were unremitting. While this might have been expected from those Indians who had refused to be part of the peace program, no one could have foreseen the wholesale going-over of peaceful Apaches to their brethren, an event that threatened to destroy the Spanish-Indian modus vivendi forever.

In the spring of 1793 word reached the presidio of a gathering of nearly one thousand Lipan and Lipiyan Apaches under the command of Pasqualillo, Vindaviyaya, and Tuchonchujato bent on destroying San Elizario. Although the expected attack did not materialize, the Lipan Apaches continued to urge all others to join them in making war on the Spaniards.[67] The following July Vidal de Lorca informed Uranga about a strike against San Elizario or on the people going to gather salt. Apaches were seeking to avenge a punitive campaign that Captain Manuel Rengel had recently led.[68]

Routine patrols led to unexpected encounters, often with violent results. An alferez by the name of Sandoval reported in late summer 1793 that troops did battle in the Sierra Blancas with Nataje Apaches who were returning from a buffalo hunt. From the scalps, he judged that eight Apaches had been killed.[69]

September brought the alarming news that the peaceful Indians established at Janos presidio had departed and joined many from the presidio of Carrizal with the idea of falling on San Elizario and El Paso.[70] In December Commandant Vidal de Lorca learned that the Lipan were again inviting all Apaches to join them. They spoke of a Spanish captain in Coahuila who had promised to furnish them with rifles. Nevertheless, the report for that month mentioned no enemy activities.[71]

Prospects for a cessation of hostilities in 1794 appeared dismal. In mid-January Vidal de Lorca informed Uranga that all the Apaches at peace established at San Elizario had gone to Barrio's camp on the opposite side of the river, where he stubbornly insisted on living, ostensibly for a gathering and dance. Vidal de Lorca had not given them written permission and feared their true purpose. Uranga was to be on the alert. He agreed to order daily scouting reports of the Apaches' movements; they reported Barrio's assertion that it would be proven that he was no liar. Ominously the scouts stated that there were some two hundred warriors and young men and one hundred women with children. Though they could not count all the children and the elderly, the total for the encampment came to between eight hundred and a thousand. Vidal de Lorca instructed Uranga to make sure that the Apaches on the other side of the river did not leave without first telling the Spaniards.[72]

The month passed in calm, but by early February, numerous livestock thefts and retaliation by the citizens were being reported. Fearing hostilities from Barrio's camp, Vidal de Lorca ordered troops from San Elizario into the field.[73]

Trouble also came from another quarter. On 23 February 1794 Vidal de Lorca alerted Uranga that all the Apaches at peace had slipped off except for the followers of Capitancillos Barrio, Mayá, and Maselchide. Vidal de Lorca assigned twenty militiamen and forty citizens from the pueblos to guard the horse herd at San Elizario and led a detachment after the Indians who had abandoned El Paso.[74]

He returned within two weeks and sent the militiamen and citizens home.[75] Before another week passed, however, he was preparing to go on campaign again. Apaches had stolen twenty horses and mules from Rafael Telles of Ysleta. In response, Vidal de Lorca summoned the thirty most experienced militiamen and citizens to participate in a twenty-day punitive expedition. He also called up as reserves another fifty men with less experience. Vidal de Lorca would go on ahead, and the men could join him as soon as they were ready.[76] In the Organ Mountains, the enemy surprised Vidal de Lorca and a fifteen-man unit. The commandant was among the fatalities recorded in the skirmish.[77]

Manuel Rengel informed Uranga from San Elizario that the Indians at peace from the El Paso area were gathered in the Guadalupe Mountains. Another large group under El Calvo was in the Sierra Obscuras. The first group was near the salines, and Rengel worried about the citizens who were planning their trip there to collect salt.[78] Within days Rengel received an order from the general command to launch a major expedition to avenge the losses suffered by the presidio of San Elizario. Sixty soldiers, including one subaltern; thirty hand-picked militiamen; and thirty Indians from El Paso were to ready themselves for a two-month campaign. They were to take flints, one hundred cartridges, and one hundred bullets. Indians were to be armed with bows, arrows, and lances. The citizens who were not named were to provide the necessary animals.[79] Before leaving on campaign, reports of Apache raiding parties arrived. Fires could be seen in the Organ Mountains and at Las Cruces, indicating the presence of the enemy.

When the army took to the field, Lieutenant José Escageda, Vidal de Lorca's successor, was left in charge of the presidio. He warned the justicias of the river pueblos in late May that peaceful Indians from San Elizario had informed him that a large number of the enemy had gathered on the other side of the river. San Elizario required the immediate assistance of thirty men from El Paso. The following month Uranga announced the appointment of Francisco Javier Bernal as a militia captain with the express duty of punishing the enemy preying on the area.[80] Meanwhile, writing from Fray Cristóbal, Rengel informed Uranga that Barrio, Mayá, Macelchide, El Calvo, and many Indians from the Guadalupe Mountains were in the Organs and might be causing problems. Uranga was to notify the commander of San Elizario.[81]

By the end of June Rengel's expedition had produced tangible results: sixty Apache prisoners delivered to San Elizario. Moreover, two warriors and Barrio's wife requested peace on his behalf; Capitancillos Mayá and Maselchide also sought terms. Nava responded pragmatically. First, he ordered Captain Rengel to continue persecuting the enemy Apaches. He considered this strategy no obstacle to making a peace treaty with those coming to solicit one in that jurisdiction. Second, he wanted verification of

the terms under which they are requesting peace, where they plan to be located, what makes them desire peace, and everything else conducive to making the judgment that they really want to live in peace without causing damages. If they request it in a way that promises permanent peace, I shall grant it under just conditions. Otherwise, they may return to their nations, where I shall persecute them continuously until they surrender or I finish them all.[82]

Shortly thereafter, Uranga reported that Barrio and Mayá had agreed to settle at San Elizario.

In August Escageda wrote to the lieutenant governor of El Paso from San Elizario to tell him that the commandant general had ordered all Apache prisoners sent to Chihuahua.[83] This measure must have contributed to the Apaches' growing resentment; having lost on the field of battle, they now had to endure the indignity of seeing their friends and relatives shipped off to captivity. Whatever their motive, the Apache Canalzoze reported in early October that some other Apaches had stolen livestock and that Barrio and Mayá had departed with their people.[84]

Antonio Vargas sounded the alarm again the following May. According to Cusichinde, four Lipiyan and Lipan Apache capitancillos had joined forces and were gathering in the Sacramento Mountains with the aim of attacking San Elizario. All the people of the pueblos were directed to guard their livestock night and day under pain of fines and possible imprisonment.[84] In early August San Elizario suffered a considerable loss. Troops discovered twenty-seven cadavers in the nearby mountains, among them the presidial soldiers Caetano Limón and José Fernández.[86]

In April 1797 word reached San Elizario that a large enemy force led by Capitancillo Arrieta was preparing to attack. He had already raided Tagourm's ranchería because he would not join in battle against the Spaniards. Manuel Rengel prepared to meet the challenge with a mounted force, but could not draw on the citizens of the El Paso district because it was planting season.[87] That summer authorities in San Elizario learned that Capitancillo Mayá, long considered at peace, was actually in league with the enemy Apaches.[88] By early August Rengel was organizing another campaign. He requested forty citizens from El Paso to accompany him, stipulating that they should be selected from among those with an aptitude for war and that they should not send peons as substitutes.[89]

Livestock thefts became an almost constant occurrence in 1798. Nava advised Lieutenant Governor Miguel Cañuelas in early summer to be on guard because of the large number of Apaches at peace under the Gila (Mimbres) capitancillo, Chafalote,[90] and others in the mountains opposite the presidio of San Elizario. In December he demanded that the commandant explain why he had assigned land to Capitancillos Arrieta and Mayá farther from San Elizario than Nava had stipulated.[91]

A large gathering of two groups of Indians from the Magdalena and San Mateo Mountains heading for San Elizario in November 1798 prompted the commanding officer of San Elizario, José María de la Riva, to ask Lieutenant Governor Cañuelas for 150 men to meet any eventuality.[92] De la Riva warned the Apaches not to come without sending ahead ten or twelve Indians who had been at peace before.

In mid-November, New Mexico Governor Fernando Chacón complained that the Apaches at peace from San Elizario were laying waste to New Mexico. One month earlier more than a hundred of them, at least eighty mounted on horseback and ten with firearms, had attacked Laguna Pueblo, carrying off 224 horses. As they fled from pursuing Pueblo Indians, the Apaches left behind telltale boxes of cigarettes, which proved they were from the peace camps. He demanded the return of the horses, even if the Apaches claimed sanctuary in San Elizario. Governor Chacón also responded to Nava's reminder to take care when denying peace to the Mescaleros, Lipiyan, and Llaneros.[93]

A new commandant at the presidio, Manuel Merino, received a warning from Nava early in 1799. Once again Indians from the Magdalena and San Mateo Mountains posed a threat to the area. Nava also ordered Merino to be alert for Apaches from San Elizario who were attacking in New Mexico. Thenceforth sanctuary would be refused to Indians who were at peace in one jurisdiction and raiding in another.[94] An apparently successful campaign was waged against these groups. Later in the year Nava wrote to the governor of New Mexico to inform him that he had ordered the commandant of San Elizario to return the prisoners to the Indians in the San Mateo, Magdalena, and Sacramento Mountains, who were to be admonished about violations of the existing peace treaty. Nava also reiterated that his 14 October 1791 regulations were still in force.[95] He ordered monthly campaigns of 150 to 200 men in June 1800 under the commandant of San Elizario, Captain Manuel de Ochoa.[96] Thereafter, small groups of Apache prisoners appeared at the presidio almost every month, year after year.[97]

THE PEACE PROGRAM AFTER NAVA

The betrayals, raids, and punitive expeditions of the eighteenth century carried over into the nineteenth. In January 1804 five peaceful capitancillos from Janos, San Buenaventura, Carrizal, San Elizario, and El Paso were planning a revolt and trying to enlist the Navajos in their confederation. The Spaniards managed to avoid disaster by successfully concluding a peace with the Navajos.[98] In April 1806 José Manrrique,[99] then in command at San Elizario, acknowledged receipt of information about enemy thefts of livestock, including horses, cattle, and oxen. A fifty-day retaliatory expedition was launched before the month was out.[100]

These occurrences did not, however, prevent some progress with the Apaches at peace. Over time those settled around the presidio of San Elizario routinely requested written permission to leave the area to go hunting.[101] Manrrique granted the lieutenant governor authority to allow Capitancillo Mayá to go hunting as far as the Robledo Mountains, with the understanding that under no circumstances was he to cross the river to the Organ Mountains. In the future the Indians were to apply in San Elizario for permission to go hunting.

When they returned from their hunts, the Apaches frequently brought with them stolen animals they had recovered from the enemy.[102] Of no less importance, they provided information on the movements of the hostile Apaches. Apaches at peace also participated in campaigns and were valued for their translation skills, knowledge of the enemy, and fighting ability.[103] Manrrique also acknowledged that Capitancillos Panchele and José had expressed their willingness to abandon their maize fields, which were already planted, to move to others near El Paso.[104] Capitancillo Concho joined those who had requested peace.[105]

Early successes notwithstanding, the program produced ambiguous results. It seemed that for every capitancillo and his people who accepted terms and settled peaceably among the river communities, another defiantly refused to give up the traditional nomadic existence. Though monthly reports listing no enemy activity were not uncommon, presidial correspondence for much of the period was punctuated by mentions of raid and retaliation.

The troops from San Elizario took to the field in August 1806 for what was to be a thirty- to thirty-five-day campaign, the results of which are unknown.[106] At the end of the month Manrrique apprised the lieutenant governor of the fact that a Mescalero Apache who would be appearing before him with a document from Manrrique was traveling to enemy territory. Manrrique indicated that he should be allowed to pass through El Paso on his return with some Apaches who were seeking peace. They were not to be impeded on their journey back to San Elizario.[107]

That winter Manrrique informed the lieutenant governor that after a large number of the enemy had slaughtered some thirty cattle stolen from the jurisdiction of El Paso, he had pursued them and killed three. Concerned that seeking revenge they would follow his tracks and attack either El Paso or San Elizario, he urged caution. He was planning to put a detachment into the field and requested fifteen men to join him on 2 December in San Elizario. They were to be supplied for thirty days, taking two strong horses in addition to their pack animals.[108]

After Apaches stole some livestock from Senecú,

Manrrique advised sending out scouts to reconnoiter. He further recommended that livestock being pastured on the other side of the river be moved to this side where they could be protected more easily.[109] In late December, Manrrique related to the lieutenant governor in El Paso the flight from San Elizario of the Apache, Fuerte, who was from Carrizal. Fuerte had escaped with women and two horses stolen from the Indians of Janos. Manrrique called for vigilance, especially in the pastures and surroundings of El Paso.[110]

Manrrique requested seven Indians from El Paso to accompany thirty soldiers from San Elizario for a projected forty days in the field in January 1807.[111] The armed contingent, under the command of Lieutenant Colonel Alberto Máynez,[112] was going out to pursue Faraón and Mescalero Apaches. Before the troops could leave their barracks, Indian raiders carried off more livestock.[113] In a March battle with Mescaleros, Manrrique lost four men.[114] From April through August, presidial troops averaged one campaign a month to punish Apaches who had stolen livestock.[115]

Nicolás Tarín, writing to the lieutenant governor of El Paso from San Elizario in October, acknowledged receipt of information that six Indians at peace and their families had fled from the Senecú area, stealing eighteen animals, which the justicia of Senecú recovered from them in the Hueco Mountains.[116] Capitancillo Panchele had provided intelligence about the number of Indians who fled Senecú. At the same time, thirteen citizens from El Paso who had been guarding the horse herd arrived in San Elizario. Tarín ordered the herd moved from the stubble of Socorro because the enemy was thought to be preparing an attack. Tarín advised the lieutenant governor that the justicia of Socorro had not yet moved the herd and that it would be a good idea to gather the Mescaleros and Llaneros from the Socorro area together to find out whether the fear was justified.[117]

The following month word reached Tarín that among the peaceful Apaches of El Paso, Dientón, who was inebriated at the time, killed Cara Negra. Seven men and two brothers of the deceased had subsequently gone after Dientón, who had fled with his family; they returned without having located him. This incident was the only one recorded for the entire period in which alcohol was involved, despite the role traditionally assigned to strong drink as a tool for breaking down Indian resistance.[118]

In late November some Apaches at peace who had been away hunting arrived in San Elizario. They brought eighty-one sheep, which were to be sent to El Paso and returned to their rightful owners. Three more sheep were being kept with the small flock in San Elizario until the lieutenant governor decided to whom they should go.[119]

Capitancillos Mayá and Panchele established themselves and their families at the presidio of San Elizario in March 1808. Nemesio Salcedo, the newly appointed commandant general, reminded the lieutenant governor that they were to stay there and request written permission to travel to El Paso or other pueblos in the district. If they traveled without papers, they would be charged with any hostilities that occurred. Obviously this requirement was observed in the breach and the implied threat was ignored.[120] By late summer the lieutenant governor had to supply twenty citizens to accompany a campaign against Indians who were fugitives from San Elizario.[121]

Still, other Apaches at peace were deemed to be important military assets. Six warriors and their families from San Elizario had been enlisted to serve as scouts on a planned campaign in northern New Mexico. Three were from the rancheria of Capitancillo Concha and three from that of Capitancillo Vizenagotán. Because the governor could not raise a sufficient force, however, they returned south. Their skill in moving through open country also made Apaches at peace valuable couriers.[122]

In February 1809 the Spaniards' worst fears came true. Some of the Indians at peace rebelled and attacked the presidio of San Elizario.[123] Then Apache raiders recorded a series of stunning thefts. They stole twenty-five head of cattle from Socorro in early April 1809 and, around the end of the month, another one hundred head from the citizens of El Paso and a herd of unspecified size from Senecú. They carried off thirty more cattle in June. Ninety-nine soldiers from the presidio of San Elizario, under the command of Alferez Joaquín Cerón, and thirty citizens from Senecú and Ysleta took to the field that month to punish the enemy.[124] Word that hostile Indians in the Organ Mountains had wounded an Indian auxiliary from the peace establishments infuriated the Spaniards. Because they continued in their obstinacy, Félix Colomo promised that he would do everything he could to punish them.[125]

Veteran campaigner Juan Francisco Granados, who had successfully warred against the Apaches in the El Paso area some nineteen years earlier, was there that summer. Perhaps his years of experience had taught him the value of caution. He acknowledged reports on enemy tracks in the El Paso area, but declined to send out troops pending further intelligence. He reacted similarly to the news that eighty Apaches had attacked men from El Paso who had gone out to bring back their cattle. A fierce battle ensued, and only five Spaniards were wounded. Granados stated that he had no troops available to pursue the enemy in the Organ Mountains.[126] His attitude may well have reflected the new reality that the Spanish military faced on the far northern frontier as a deadly new foe replaced an older one.

THE DEFENSE OF NEW MEXICO

With the purchase of the Louisiana Territory from France in 1803, the United States touched on Spanish territory at the Rocky Mountains, though the exact boundary, including the status of Texas, remained indefinite until resolved by treaty in 1819. Don Pedro Baptista Pino, the New Mexico deputy to the Spanish Cortes, warned of the imminent danger—averted to that point—of Spain's provinces falling prey, one by one, to the United States.

> In fact they have already tried by offering commercial advantages and easy and protective laws, as an inducement [to the New Mexicans] to unite their valuable section of territory with the Louisiana Purchase, which borders on our domain. But neither by this means, nor by threats posed by the construction of forts near our borders, nor by arming hostile tribes opposed to us, have they managed to do anything but receive setbacks that frustrated their plans every time. [127]

This dangerous presence was felt in San Elizario by 1806, as interlopers from the young United States arrived.[128] Ellis Bean, the lone survivor of Philip Nolan's 1800 expedition to eastern Texas, spent time in the lockup at San Elizario.[129] Spanish officials arrested Captain Zebulon Montgomery Pike of the United States Army at the headwaters of the Rio Grande above Santa Fe and charged him with entering Spanish territory illegally. Pike was brought to the El Paso del Norte area under heavy guard in March 1807 and escorted to the presidio of San Elizario. He remained for three days, taking note of the hospitality of the people and the productivity of the area. He also reported that there were many Apaches living around the presidio under treaty arrangements governing Spanish-Apache relations that Pike found commendable. "These people appeared to be perfectly independent in their manners," wrote Pike, "and were the only savages I saw in the Spanish dominions whose spirit was not humbled, whose necks were not bowed to the yoke of their invaders."[130]

Pike was then escorted to Chihuahua for questioning. Although his papers were confiscated, he managed to hide his journal. When published later in Philadelphia after his release, his comments regarding the commercial opportunities to be found in Spanish New Mexico received considerable attention in the United States.

A number of other Anglo-Americans were soon reported in New Mexico, proof that their appearances were not isolated cases but the beginning of a significant trend—the Anglo-American advance into Spanish New Mexico. In May 1810 Commandant General Nemesio Salcedo, warning of the potential threat that Joseph Napoleon posed, sent orders to the interim governor of New Mexico to detain all foreigners and send them to the presidio of San Elizario.[131] When a party of seven men from the upper Louisiana Territory arrived in Santa Fe, their goods were seized, and they were sent to San Elizario for a two-year confinement. A larger party in 1812 suffered the same fate.[132]

After the outbreak of the war for Mexican independence in 1810, San Elizario became a vital link between Santa Fe and Chihuahua. In New Mexico the presidio of Santa Fe was entrusted with the defense of the province against any and all potential enemies, whether hostile Indian groups, insurgent sympathizers, or Anglo-Americans. The presidio of San Elizario was to be maintained at full strength to keep the communication lines open between Chihuahua and Santa Fe and support the Santa Fe garrison with soldiers, arms, horses, and supplies whenever needed.[133]

The liberal Constitution of 1812, drafted in the Spanish port city of Cadiz, was proclaimed in Chihuahua on 1 November 1813. Representatives of the presidial and mobile companies were present to swear allegiance. Two from San Elizario were on hand for the event: the armorer, Ignacio Hernández, and a private, José Berrú. For their trouble, and perhaps in the spirit of celebration, the treasury provided each man with two reales.[134]

Following the triumph of royalist forces, San Elizario served in a supporting role, furnishing assistance and supplies to the presidio of Santa Fe. Accounts from the treasury in Chihuahua reveal information about the deployment of troops from San Elizario during this period.

Entries for disbursements indicate that, while several soldiers were assigned duty in Chihuahua, most were on record as being in San Elizario. Noteworthy is the fact that a picket from the Third Company of Volunteers was attached to the presidio of San Elizario, at least for the last half of 1816. A single entry relates to the Apaches. On 3 October Corporal Pedro Albídrez received three hundred pesos to purchase blankets for distribution among the Apaches at peace at San Elizario.[135]

From 1818 until Mexican independence in 1821, troops from San Elizario escorted the annual supply caravan to Santa Fe. According to an 1818 document, Isidro Rey was the commandant of the presidio of San Elizario. Under his command were a first lieutenant, two alfereces, a chaplain, an armorer, three sergeants, a drummer, six corporals, five cadets, and seventy-six privates. In support of the New Mexico garrisons, Commandant Rey established a military escort known as the New Mexico Detachment, whose function was to convey food, clothing, arms, and ammunition. A San Elizario presidial muster of 1819 lists thirty-two men out of a total of ninety-two, or one-third of the complement, serving in New Mexico—a sergeant, a corporal, two riflemen, and twenty-eight privates. Each year from 1818 to 1821, a presidial escort made an expedition to New Mexico to transport shipments of food—wheat, corn, mutton, and sugar; and clothing—jackets, shirts, shoes; soap; and gunpowder.

These provisions were carried to the Spanish garrisons of Santa Fe, Albuquerque, and Taos.[136]

A principal Santa Fe official involved in these supply operations was don Pedro de Armendáriz, a high-ranking administrator who had been a first lieutenant at the presidio of San Elizario. He was interested in New Mexico's economic development as well as its defense, and in 1819-20 he obtained two large land grants, known as the Valverde and the San Cristóbal tracts, located just south of Socorro, New Mexico, at the northern edge of the Jornada del Muerto on the main route from San Elizario to Santa Fe. Although this fertile valley supported a population increase for a while, repeated Indian attacks forced its abandonment following considerable loss of life and property. In a letter Armendáriz wrote to the governor of New Mexico, Facundo Melgares, on 1 November 1821, he refers to a shipment of goods from the presidio of San Elizario to the post of Valverde, an indication of the special relationship between the presidio and the outposts of New Mexico during the Mexican independence period.[137]

Meanwhile Spanish policy toward Anglo-Americans in New Mexico remained unchanged. In 1815 a group of twenty-six Anglo-American traders and trappers were seized, relieved of their goods, confined for a time, and sent back to the United States. Not until 1821, when a revolution overthrew Spanish rule in New Mexico, were Anglo-American traders and their merchandise given a warmer reception in Santa Fe.[138]

Presidial soldiers from San Elizario campaigned in New Mexico against Apaches, Navajos, and Comanches.[139] The latter group proved to be an implacable foe who also attacked the Apaches at peace established at San Elizario.[140] Apaches from a number of groups, including Faraones and Mescaleros, settled nearby. While in all likelihood they continued to be culturally Apache, those born and raised in close proximity to the Spaniards probably knew much of the latter's customs and language.[141] By mid-1815 many of the capitancillos, including Pansels, Papel, and Farincaya, and their followers had left the San Elizario area. They wandered upriver and settled near Belen, New Mexico, for a time. They were hungry and suffering from an epidemic, probably smallpox, that lasted through the summer months.[142] There is no indication that those groups returned to San Elizario, although peaceful Apaches continued to reside there until the end of the colonial period and beyond. Some Apaches at peace were living there in the winter of 1819 when erstwhile peaceful Comanches attacked them.[143]

In July 1820 instructions for the selection of deputies to the Spanish Cortes arrived. Representatives were to be chosen from a district comprising the presidios of San Elizario, Janos, San Buenaventura, Carrizal, El Norte, El Príncipe, Conchos, and the cuartel of Namiquipa.[144] As it happened, though, their choice was of no consequence, for in September 1821 Agustín de Iturbide emerged victorious in Mexico. Mexican independence was established not by a social revolutionary such as Miguel Hidalgo, who initiated the movement in 1810, but by this astute army officer who organized a conservative movement to liberate his country from a liberal regime in Spain. The success of Iturbide's movement in September 1821 brought an end to three hundred years of Spanish rule in New Spain. The conservative implementation of Iturbide's plan for the future of Mexico, of course, differed widely from those ideals held by Hidalgo and Morelos—a Mexico ruled by all those born in Mexico, regardless of race or class, whether criollo, mestizo, or Indian. For that reason Mexican independence is celebrated on 16 September, the anniversary of Hidalgo's Grito de Dolores of 1810, rather than commemorating any particular event in 1821 associated with Iturbide. Despite the advent of independence, San Elizario maintained continuity with its past; the retired alferez, José Antonio Arce, was named captain of the presidio in the new state of Chihuahua.[145]

THE MEXICAN PERIOD, 1821–1848

INDEPENDENT MEXICO—THE EL PASO AREA

INDEPENDENT MEXICO—THE EL PASO AREA

With the establishment of Mexican independence from Spain in 1821, what is now the American Southwest became a part of the Mexican nation. After a brief rule by Agustín de Iturbide, the liberator of Mexico, a new constitution created a federal republic roughly patterned after that of the United States. The Constituent Act of the Federation, promulgated on 31 January 1824, organized the Mexican nation out of the territory formerly known as New Spain. According to the terms of Article 7, the provinces of Chihuahua, Durango, and New Mexico went together to form the Interior State of the North. On 6 July 1824 the states of Chihuahua and Durango and the territory of New Mexico replaced the Interior State of the North. This action removed the El Paso del Norte area from the jurisdiction of New Mexico for the first time. The five settlements of El Paso del Norte; San Lorenzo, Senecú, Ysleta, and Socorro, formerly under New Mexico jurisdiction, and the presidio of San Elizario, formerly a part of Nueva Vizcaya, were incorporated into the state of Chihuahua. The Federal Republic was organized into states that were divided into districts called *partidos*. Each partido had a *cabecera*, or principal town. A *jefe político* presided over the cabecera and served as president of an *ayuntamiento* in towns with a population exceeding two thousand, such as El Paso. This town council consisted of two *alcaldes constitutionales*, three *regidores*, and a *síndico*. *Juntas municipales* governed smaller communities having a population between eight hundred and two thousand people. Communities of fewer than eight hundred people were attached to the next larger town for administrative matters. As capital of the Partido del Paso, El Paso had an ayuntamiento, while San Lorenzo, Socorro, Ysleta, and San Elizario each had municipal juntas, which in practice were also often referred to as ayuntamientos. Although elections were regularly held, the landowning and mercantile aristocracy of El Paso del Norte dominated the local political structure. On 1 October 1824 the federal constitution was adopted.[1]

The civil community of San Elizario, which had begun to emerge out of the shadow of the original presidial population, anticipated some of these changes before the Mexican congress formally adopted them. By late 1823 Marcelino Escageda was *alcalde constitutional,* president of its municipal corporation, and *subdelegado* of the *puesto*, or post, of San Elizario. José Antonio Arroyo, the dominant political figure of his day, followed him in office, becoming both *alcalde conciliador* and subdelegado of the puesto of San Elizario in 1825–26 and again in 1836. Nemesio Márquez occupied the post of alcalde in 1833, as did José Joaquín Gutiérrez the next year. Although the historical record is incomplete, it is possible to demonstrate that changes dictated at the national level were being felt at the local level in San Elizario as well.[2]

The population of the El Paso area at the beginning of the Mexican period was about eight thousand. El Paso del Norte was the largest of the five settlements with a greater number of residents than all the others combined. A flourishing agriculture existed that featured a fertile soil mixed with a sandy loam and irrigated by a network of acequias. The principal products were corn, wheat, fruits, and vegetables; and the quality and flavor of the grapes, wine, and brandy the vineyards produced ranked with the best, according to almost every official who visited the area. With the exception of the *ejidos*, the communal holdings of the mission Indians, wealthy *paseños* owned most of the land in the form of haciendas, ranches, or farms. Beginning in the 1830s the Chihuahua trade along the camino real, a natural extension of the Santa Fe trade with Missouri that had begun a decade earlier, supplemented the area's agricultural base.[3]

Traditionally agriculture, stock-raising, and trade provided the area with a large degree of self-sufficiency, the Rio Grande serving as a spinal cord that unified the region. The capricious river frequently overflowed its banks, particularly in late spring, causing untold damage to fields, crops, livestock, and adobe structures. In 1830–31 the rampaging river formed a new channel south of the old one, placing Ysleta, Socorro, and the presidio of San Elizario on an island some twenty miles in length and two to four miles in width. For the remainder of the Mexican period this area was called "la Isla," or "the Island." The Rio Grande continued to flow primarily in the new channel, and eventually water ceased to flow in the Río Viejo, or old riverbed. The flooding washed away the Ysleta and Socorro Missions, but in time they were replaced on higher ground by the present structures.[4]

In 1823 the ayuntamiento of El Paso del Norte voted to maintain the existing peace establishment for the Apaches, including the rations program for the twelve hundred Apache settlers. The reaction of individual presidial soldiers at the nearby presidio of San Elizario to Mexican independence must have been varied. Some of those from the presidio of San Elizario, probably most, cast their lot with the land of their birth and fought against Spain. Provisions were made for those who had opted to fight neither Spain nor Mexico. A directive from the Secretariat of War and the Navy in February 1825 stated that former soldiers holding the rank of sergeant and below who had deserted but failed to join the Army of the Three Guarantees either before or after independence would be given two months to enlist without any marks against them.[5]

Major legislation regarding presidios handed down in March 1826 provided for a presidial system to defend the

northern territories in the Mexican republic. The state of Chihuahua was to have five presidial companies, located at Chihuahua, Janos, San Elizario, El Norte, and San Buenaventura. The capital was to have the largest company, with a complement of 141; Janos, San Elizario, and El Norte were to have 96; and San Buenaventura was to have 72. The total yearly expenditure for San Elizario was set at 26,894 pesos.[6] In April the ayuntamiento in El Paso voiced its approval for a complement to the presidio of San Elizario consisting of a captain, a lieutenant, two alfereces, a chaplain, an armorer, three sergeants, a drummer, six corporals, and eighty privates. José Antonio de Arce was named captain of the presidio.[7]

MEXICAN-APACHE RELATIONS, 1821–1840

During the 1820s Mexican relations with the Apaches were based largely on the Spanish colonial view that Apaches in time could accept and learn the Hispanics' way of life. Presidio commanders were instructed to persuade the Apaches to remain in one place, support themselves by their own labor, learn agricultural techniques, and send their sons to local schools. Conflicts and hostilities were kept to a minimum for a time, and no major Mexican military campaigns in Chihuahua were ordered during the decade following Mexican independence. There was even an absence of local punitive expeditions against Apaches that would have resulted in deaths and incited Apache revenge.[8]

José Agustín de Escudero provided remarkably detailed figures for the establishments of Apaches at peace in Chihuahua and Sonora. Although there is some question among scholars regarding the accuracy of his work, and it seems certain that these numbers refer to a period many years before his work was published in 1834, he may well have had access to sources since lost. At any rate, his is the only information of its kind at hand for San Elizario during the period and therefore merits attention. Unfortunately, Escudero mentioned only Faraón Apaches in association with San Elizario, though from the names of the capitancillos he listed, it is clear that other groups were also involved.[9]

Apaches at Peace at San Elizario

Capitancillos	Men	Women and Children	Total
Papel	80	229	309
Bigotes	90	248	338
Organo	18	51	69
Nataesyá	10	37	47
Isquinédiseñé	14	45	59
José	8	22	30
Tacintayé	32	60	92
Yescas	16	71	87
Intaé	27	92	119
Muyá	17	35	52
Total	**312**	**890**	**1,202**

Escudero stated that these Indians were given modest weekly rations to provide for their families. Every other year some articles of clothing were given to the capitancillos or to Indians who had distinguished themselves through their loyalty and bravery while on campaign, which they frequently did, as guides and auxiliaries.[10] Escudero does not cite a source for these figures, which Griffen reckons are from the mid-1820s, at least with respect to Janos. There are no records in the Juárez Archive that either corroborate or contradict them, but the names of the leaders makes 1825 seem plausible for San Elizario as well. If the numbers are accurate, San Elizario had become the most important center for Apaches at peace, accommodating almost half of all those associated with the presidios in Chihuahua and Sonora.[11]

Major changes in Mexican-Apache relations, however, occurred during the 1830s. On the grounds that the Apaches were costing the Chihuahua government too much and were not doing enough to support themselves, Commandant General José Joaquín Calvo of Chihuahua ordered the termination of the rations program. Although Mexican officials hoped that this action would force idle Apaches back to work, the immediate result was the renewal of Apache raids that ended a decade of peaceful relations. The Apache colony at the presidio of San Elizario soon drifted away to the New Mexico hinterland. The Chihuahua government concluded that the Apaches had broken the peace treaties and declared war on them.[12]

In the spring of 1832 Mexican strategy called for a decisive blow that would bring the Apaches to their knees and force them to sue for peace. From 21 through 23 May Mexican troops under the command of the eminent *paseño,* José Ignacio Ronquillo, battled the Apaches on the Gila River. They killed 32 warriors, wounded 51 more, and retrieved 140 horses. A month later at Santa Rita del Cobre a truce was arranged that assigned specific designated territories to four groups of Apaches, with the Mescaleros receiving land extending from the presidio of San Elizario to the Sacramento Mountains. In August Apache chieftains and Captain Ronquillo signed peace treaties, but when they proved to be brittle, Mexicans quickly assumed that Apaches across the northern frontier were in rebellion.[13]

With the resumption of Apache raids that grew in intensity during the 1830s, the settlers in the El Paso area continued to live in a state of terror, never knowing when the "Mongols of the desert" would strike and in what numbers. Their principal target was livestock; they would go to any length to obtain it, and they would destroy anything that stood in their way. C. L. Sonnichsen writes that pieces of glass have been found in some of the old adobe structures in the El Paso area, placed there by settlers to prevent the Apaches from sawing out a portion of wall with a rawhide rope in order to steal the livestock. At camouflaging their position beside a road or concealing themselves behind boulders and striking down Mexicans with arrows and lances smeared in rattlesnake venom, they had no superiors.[14]

In August 1832 Commandant General Calvo established three military zones extending from south to north across the state of Chihuahua. The Advanced Guard was in the south, the Center Guard in the middle, and the Rear Guard in the north, the state's first line of defense against the hostile Indians of the northern frontier. With headquarters in El Paso del Norte, it consisted of the permanent active companies at El Paso del Norte; the mines of Santa Rita del Cobre; and the presidios of Janos, San Buenaventura, Carrizal, and San Elizario. It also embraced the civilian militias of El Paso del Norte, Galeana, Durango, and New Mexico.[15]

By 1836 José Ignacio Ronquillo had reorganized the personnel and equipment of the presidio of San Elizario. Its new complement consisted of Captain Ronquillo, a lieutenant, an alferez, a sergeant, six corporals, and eighty-two privates. The military equipment included muskets, lances, arrows, cartridges, stones, and mounts. The area's defenses also included the cavalry company of El Paso del Norte with its total of ninety-two under the command of Captain José Francisco del Barrio.[16]

The presidio of San Elizario answered the call to help put down an armed rebellion in New Mexico in 1838. Twenty-six men, including Captain Tomás Zuloaga, joined a force of 167 soldiers under the command of Lieutenant Colonel Caetano Justiniani, the military commander of the El Paso jurisdiction. Arriving in Santa Fe in January, the Mexican regular forces met the rebels at Pojoaque on the twenty-seventh. There, and in skirmishes on the twenty-eighth and twenty-ninth with the fleeing New Mexicans, troops from San Elizario participated in a resounding victory, resulting in the deaths of 57 rebels, both Indians and citizens. According to the service record of one of the soldiers who participated in these engagements, the national government rewarded him with a bonus and a promotion after his return to San Elizario.[17]

Troubles in New Mexico notwithstanding, Captain Ronquillo's principal objective was a peace treaty with the Mescaleros. He succeeded in signing a number of agreements with the chieftains of neighboring rancherias and was highly confident that a major show of force by a sizable army sent by the commandant general would bring the Mescaleros to terms. This, however, had but little chance of success since the Apaches were now raiding central and southern Chihuahua. To make matters worse, the Comanches were intensifying their activities. In a word, Chihuahua's defenses were in ruins and its economy a shambles. It was only a matter of time, concluded Chihuahua officials, before Apaches would be camping outside the state capital. A helpless and desperate Chihuahua government turned to foreign mercenaries to solve their problems.[18]

Santiago (James) Kirker, an Irishman turned Mexican, a trapper, hunter, and explorer, was perhaps the most notorious of the paid killers of the period. Kirker knew the Apaches well, for he had sold them muskets, pistols, powder, and knives and joined them on raids; he could use his friendship with the Apaches to exploit them. In 1839 the Chihuahua government formed La Sociedad de Guerra Contra los Bárbaros (The Society for War Against the Barbarians), placed Kirker in charge, and offered him

100,000 pesos to bring the Indian problem under control. Known as "the king of New Mexico," Kirker, who could match the Apaches in marksmanship, horsemanship, treachery, and torture, led a party of scalp hunters who collected a huge bounty in Chihuahua during the next two years. George Ruxton, the English traveler, was impressed with the fruits of one of Kirker's campaigns—namely, the trophies he saw "dangling in front of the cathedral." Some Mexican officials, however, thought that Kirker's exploits were too costly; others considered them distasteful and despicable, while still others said they were counterproductive, since both Apache and Comanche raids were on the increase by 1841. By this time the Chihuahua government was convinced that a different approach to the Apache problem should be attempted. Having lost his Chihuahua support, Kirker joined his former adversaries and became known as "the chief of the Apache Nation."[19]

SAN ELIZARIO BECOMES A TOWN— THE 1830S

The historiography of the borderlands holds that the Spanish presidio often served as a nucleus for the development of a town. The lure of the presidio payroll, the promise of military protection, and the offer of a government subsidy, writes Max Moorhead, were all potent inducements. Thus scores of towns developed in the shelter of these far-flung bastions. Most of them outlived by many decades the garrison forts that spawned them, and many of them still survive. San Elizario is a case in point.[20]

The rations program that Spain initiated and Mexico continued brought laborers to the area to produce livestock, grains, fruits, and vegetables for the Apache colony at the presidio of San Elizario. Several hundred Mexican workers had come to the area by 1831 when the rations program was terminated and Apache raids began again. The presidio had a population of 432 in 1833, and in the following year the ayuntamiento of El Paso del Norte ordered a census of the civilian population to determine the number of adult males available for military service. The resulting census of 1834 recorded a total population of 768 for the San Elizario community, of whom 313 were adult males. Each was judged for his suitability for the infantry or the cavalry.[21]

The loss of Texas led to a change in government in Mexico. A conservative constitution, promulgated on 31 December 1836, was put into effect on 20 March of the following year. With the new government came territorial reorganization. Departments replaced states; the president appointed governors of departments. The governor, in turn, appointed *prefectos* and reviewed the appointments of *subprefectos* and *jueces de paz* in consultation with a *junta departmental*. Departments were divided into districts called *prefecturas* under a prefecto's leadership; El Paso was one such district. The prefecto served a four-year term and resided in the cabecera of his *prefectura*. Subprefectos resided in the cabecera of the partido, the most important community in the subdistrict. Subprefectos recommended individuals deemed appropriate to serve as jueces de paz. Ayuntamientos were authorized for communities of at least 4,000.[22] These structural changes were eventually implemented in San Elizario. By 1843 Gregorio Gándara was serving as juez de paz there. The ayuntamiento remained, but it no longer possessed the authority it had enjoyed during the 1820s.[23]

An important document of Lower Valley history is the census of 1841. Much more comprehensive than the other censuses of the Mexican period, this one includes the total number of settlers in Ysleta, Socorro, and San Elizario, with ages, marital status, occupations, and the heads of households. The total population of the three settlements was 2,850. Socorro was the largest with 1,101, San Elizario was second with 1,018 (up from 768 in 1834), and Ysleta last with 731 (456 Spanish and 275 Indian). There were 229 heads of families for Socorro, 195 for San Elizario, and 157 for Ysleta (100 Spanish and 57 Indian). The average family size for both Spanish and Indian was 5. Most heads of households were farmworkers, followed by servants. San Elizario also had a cook, a shoemaker, a tailor, a carpenter, and several foremen. The two-room adobe structure was the pattern for housing, and poverty was widespread. Thus by the 1830s the presidio had spawned a town, which preserved the historic name of San Elizario for future generations even after the presidio came to its end in 1844.[24]

THE PRESIDIO'S LAST YEARS, 1842–1844

In July 1840 Francisco García Conde assumed the position of commandant general of Chihuahua, charged with the responsibility of repairing the state's shattered economy and defenses. Mercenaries such as Santiago Kirker, who had been employed to bring the Apache problem under control, had produced a number of scalps, but otherwise exacerbated the situation and provoked intensified Apache raiding throughout the state. The dedicated and energetic García Conde called on the towns to assume the responsibility for local defense. They were to recruit manpower, establish cavalry and infantry companies, list available weapons and equipment, and contribute financially to the defense effort. Finally, García Conde and the Chihuahua officials agreed to change the state's basic Apache policy from all-out war to all-out peace.[25]

The response of the towns to García Conde's orders was encouraging. On 18 September 1840 the six towns in the Partido del Paso submitted the following report on the number of men, firearms, arrows, and horses available for military service:

	Men	Firearms	Arrows	Horses
Villa del Paso	1232	430	802	250
Real de San Lorenzo	60	14	46	9
Pueblo de Senecú	106	23	83	23
Pueblo de Ysleta	126	41	85	49
Pueblo de Socorro	126	68	68	39
Puesto de San Elizario	129	94	35	50
Totals	1779	670	1119	420 [26]

The archival records of the El Paso–Ciudad Juárez area reveal that officials in the 1830s and 1840s were well informed about events in Mexico, Texas, and New Mexico. The newspaper of the state government of Chihuahua arrived regularly in El Paso del Norte, and handwritten copies were often made for the downriver settlements. Residents learned of the outbreak of hostilities in Texas in October 1835 and the establishment of the Texas republic in 1836. Mexican officials issued frequent appeals in the ensuing years for personal sacrifices and financial contributions to defend the Mexican nation against "the perfidious Texans." In the Juárez Archive, for example, there is a fifty-page manuscript dated 1841 entitled "Documentos relativos a la contribución personal impuesta y recaudada para los gastos de la guerra contra la invasión texana (Documents concerning the personal contribution imposed and collected for the expenses of the war against the Texan invasion)." The five towns—Villa del Paso, Real de San Lorenzo, Senecú, Ysleta, and Socorro, and the Puesto de San Elizario—contributed 739 pesos. The 1,244 residents of San Elizario contributed another 31 pesos.[27]

Mexican fears of further violations of its national territory were substantiated when it was learned that the Texan-Santa Fe Expedition had invaded New Mexico in late 1841. President Mirabeau B. Lamar, who dreamed of extending the Republic of Texas to the Pacific, initiated this project. Having received reports that Mexican rule in New Mexico was weak and unpopular, Lamar was led to believe that the residents there would welcome a Texas commercial-military expedition that would establish profitable trade relations with Santa Fe merchants and erect a government under the authority of Texas. Thus Texas's ambitious claim to the Rio Grande as its southern and western boundary would be realized.[28]

The expedition of 50 merchants and 270 troops that left Austin in June 1841 was a disaster. George Wilkins Kendall, who was editor of the *New Orleans Picayune* and had accompanied the group in anticipation of a vacation, vividly recounted in his narrative the heat, hunger, thirst, wild Indians, poor leadership, and lack of discipline they experienced. Instead of the welcome they expected in New Mexico, the men encountered determined resistance under the leadership of the governor, Manuel Armijo. The exhausted Texans were in no condition to fight, and the 172 surviving members of the expedition were taken prisoner. On the next day, 17 October 1841, they began the long march to Mexico City. In New Mexico, where Mexican anger was extremely intense, the Texas prisoners were manacled, tortured, and starved; the *cura* of El Paso del Norte, Ramón Ortiz, extended to them the only kindnesses they received on the entire trip.[29]

From the Mexican point of view, the Texan-Santa Fe Expedition was denounced as a foreign invasion of Mexican soil, and its members were therefore enemies of the Mexican nation. Mexican historian Carlos María Bustamante insisted that Anglo-Americans in New Mexico had instigated the affair and he urged Governor Armijo to organize an expedition for the reconquest of Texas. Otherwise, he said, New Mexico would undoubtedly be invaded again, if not by the Texans then by the Anglo-Americans, who were plotting to make New Mexico a part of the United States. Bustamante's allegations proved to be prophetic.[30]

Although during 1841 Commandant General García Conde consistently emphasized that the warring, raiding Apaches, who were destroying the state's principal economic activities, were the primary threat, he quickly changed his mind after the Texan invasion of New Mexico and adopted a conciliatory attitude regarding the Apaches. The Mescaleros of New Mexico indicated their willingness to cooperate in a peace program on the condition that it included a rations provision. Chief José María María then approved a treaty and sent his acceptance to the presidio of San Elizario. By the end of June 1841 he and his people were living in peace in the El Paso area, and the Apache group at the presidio began receiving their rations every two weeks. In September and October Mexicans reported that tranquility continued at El Paso and nearby settlements where Mescaleros and some Mimbreños and Gileños were living. For the next two and a half years, from September 1842 to February 1845, only a few Apache raids struck the central part of the state of Chihuahua. To be sure, there were conflicts on the frontier over minor thefts of cattle or consumption of alcohol, but all remained within manageable bounds.[31]

A desperate Chihuahua government sought an Apache peace agreement primarily because a much greater threat had emerged with the deteriorating relations between Texas and Mexico, with each raiding the other's territory for retaliation and revenge. A second Texan invasion of New Mexico in the spring of 1843 sought to capture the Mexican caravans on the Santa Fe Trail. The expedition defeated the vanguard Governor Manuel Armijo sent, but failed in its objective when a United States force intervened. Thoroughly enraged by this Texas action, and fearing others in the immediate future, Armijo sent an urgent request for reinforcements to Commandant General José Mariano Monterde of Chihuahua.[32]

In Chihuahua the Apache peace still prevailed, so that Commandant General Monterde, who no doubt viewed New Mexico as Mexico's first line of defense, quickly responded. He ordered an entire infantry battalion, a total of 360 officers and men from the capital, along with 391 from the presidios, to move north. In June 77 men from the presidio of San Elizario joined the expeditionary force bound for New Mexico. Among them were 67 privates, a captain, a lieutenant, an alferez, a first sergeant, a bugler, 6 corporals, and 2 cadets. In addition, 3 privates were on duty that month in Chihuahua. After the departure of the troops, there remained only 20 men in San Elizario out of a 90-man company.[33] The previous month, 60 officers and men had been on active duty at San Elizario, with another 29 serving in Chihuahua.[34]

Even though the Texan invasion failed to reach the gates of Santa Fe, many of the men from Chihuahua presidial companies remained on garrison duty in the New Mexican capital. A listing of all the companies serving in

Santa Fe as of December 1843 indicated that 61 officers and men from San Elizario were present.[35] A similar document for the month of January 1844 showed a total of 13 men, the highest ranking of them an alferez on active duty in San Elizario, with a like number of horses.[36] In April of that same year, only 5 soldiers, all of whom were receiving funds in El Paso, remained from the presidio: Anastacio López, Pablo Montes, Francisco Luján, Eustaquio Olguín, and José Perú.[37] Thus, that venerable institution, the presidio of San Elizario, came to an end after fifty years of service on the northern frontier, eventually falling into ruins. In Santa Fe, the men from San Elizario were apparently involved in only, routine activities of a military post. As late as the end of October 1845, they appear sporadically in New Mexico records as perpetrators or victims of petty crimes, petitioners for permission to marry, and, occasionally, deserters.[38]

Meanwhile, the peace treaties with the Apaches between 1842 and 1844 afforded the town of San Elizario an opportunity to update its population count. The census of 1844 listed the adults (by name) and children of its two residential districts. In Section 1 there were 104 adults and 359 children for a total of 463; in Section 2 there were 202 adults and 207 children for a total of 409. The total population was 872, a decline of more than a 100 in three years.[39]

By early 1845 it was evident that the peace program

initiated in 1842 was winding down. Tensions had mounted, followed by the renewal of raids and assaults, with both Mexicans and Apaches accusing the other of violating the peace agreements. Some Apaches went to the El Paso area to warn authorities there that five to six hundred warriors, among whom were Llaneros and Jicarillas as well as Mescaleros, were on their way to a large reunion at a place upriver from Doña Ana. The prefect of El Paso del Norte was concerned not so much with immediate hostilities as he was with the shortage of resources that might make it impossible to provide rations for such a large group. Such a scarcity might provoke further violence. When the Chihuahua government learned of these threats, it ordered the officials in the El Paso area to bolster local defenses and arrest all Apaches involved in criminal behavior.[40]

It has been noted that since 1840 the six towns of the El Paso district had assumed an ever increasing responsibility for their own defense. In 1845 they issued the following report relating to manpower and weapons:

	Men	Firearms	Arrows	Horses
Cabecera del Paso	1024	440	251	58
Pueblo del Real	125	23	60	5
Pueblo de Senecú	190	34	59	11
Pueblo de Ysleta	114	36	78	17
Pueblo de Socorro	230	71	122	33
Pueblo de San Elizario	113	73	5	69
Totals	**1796**	**677**	**575**	**193** [41]

On 31 May 1846 the town of San Elizario prepared a report listing the names and ages of its military personnel in three categories: those with firearms—89; those with arrows—13; and those without weapons—88. At that very moment not only were Apaches and Comanches raiding the area, but the United States had also declared war and was preparing to invade Mexico.[42]

THE DONIPHAN EXPEDITION OF 1846

After the United States annexed Texas in March 1845, Mexico broke diplomatic relations, and the threat of war became imminent. With the outbreak of hostilities in the disputed lower Rio Grande Valley, the United States declared war against Mexico in May 1846. The major offensives were directed toward northern Mexico and New Mexico, although Chihuahua eventually became a third area of conflict by reason of the extensive American economic investment there during the previous decade. James Magoffin, a veteran Chihuahua merchant, served in General Stephen W. Kearny's army, whose objective was the conquest of New Mexico. Magoffin succeeded in convincing Governor Armijo that armed resistance to American forces would be both unwise and futile. As a result, on 18 August 1846 Kearny's army entered Santa Fe unopposed without firing a shot or spilling a drop of blood.[43]

In August 1846 Angel Trías, whose anti American sentiments were well known, became governor of Chihuahua. Keenly aware that the news was ominous and the situation desperate, Trías nevertheless went about his task with zeal and determination. Sebastián Bermúdez, the prefect of El Paso del Norte, advised the governor that despite the loss of Santa Fe, the residents of the area were patriotic, loyal, and determined to prevent American forces from trampling on the soil of Chihuahua. On 26 September 1846 Governor Trías forwarded a note outlining a defensive strategy that the Chihuahua authorities had previously approved. The highest priority, said the governor, was the defense of El Paso del Norte. A squadron of two hundred cavalry was to be sent to reinforce the local militia.[44]

James Magoffin, who had played an important role in the bloodless conquest of Santa Fe, logically assumed that he could win Chihuahua in the same manner—through negotiation and persuasion rather than by force of arms. If satisfactory arrangements could be made with the Chihuahua officials, American merchants in Chihuahua jails could be released and business conditions would return to normal. Magoffin thus hoped to convince his many influential Mexican friends in Chihuahua that they had as much to gain by negotiating a peaceful settlement as the Americans did.[45]

In early September 1846 James Magoffin and his party began their march down the Rio Grande in the hope that an understanding with the Mexican officials could be reached and peace restored. The juez de paz of Doña Ana detained Magoffin and four others, however, and ordered them escorted to El Paso del Norte where they were arrested. All Magoffin's wagons, equipment, and papers were inventoried in El Paso del Norte, and he and his friends, highly suspect in the eyes of the Mexican officials, were sent under heavy guard to confinement at the presidio of Carrizal.[46]

By mid-December 1846 a sizable Mexican force under the command of Captain Antonio Ponce de León had assembled in El Paso del Norte to halt the advance of Colonel Alexander Doniphan's army of rough-and-ready Missouri volunteers. They met on 25 December 1846 at the Battle of Brazito (which the Mexicans call Temascalitos), 28 miles northwest of El Paso del Norte. The

Mexican troops, who had been confident of victory, were routed in a clash lasting about thirty minutes. The Mexicans reportedly misinterpreted a bugle call, which left them confused, demoralized, and at the mercy of a strong American charge.[47]

On 27 December American forces entered El Paso del Norte and arrested several Mexicans for anti-American activities, including the prefect, Sebastián Bermúdez, and Father Ramón Ortiz, who had been so hospitable toward the prisoners of the Texan-Santa Fe Expedition. During a February 1847 visit to El Paso del Norte, eighteen-year-old Susan Magoffin (James Magoffin's sister-in-law) recorded the opinions of José Ignacio Ronquillo, paseño aristocrat and former captain of the presidio of San Elizario:

> Don Ygnacio is a second George Washington in his *appearance*, and is altogether a great admirer of the man whose name is ever dear to the hearts of the American; he says the course Mr. Polk is persuing [sic] in regard to this war, is entirely against the principals [sic] of Washington, which were to remain at home, encourage all home improvements, to defend our rights *there* against the incroachments [sic] of others, and never to invade the territory of an other nation.[48]

Doniphan's army remained in El Paso del Norte the entire month of January 1847, since the colonel was still unclear about his next assignment and in need of reinforcements and artillery. There were a number of Apache raids, but the men soon became restless and bored by

inactivity, which led to depression, drunkenness, dissipation, and rioting. The greatest tragedy of the American occupation of El Paso del Norte in 1846–47, however, was the destruction of a portion of the municipal archive, as soldiers quartered in government buildings used manuscripts to light their candles.[49]

On 30 December two officers in Doniphan's army, Major William Gilpin and Captain John W. Reid, visited San Elizario. They found the old presidio deserted and concluded that a large force had been stationed there before the battle. A number of bloody bandages were discovered, indicating that Mexicans wounded in battle had received medical attention there. One cannon and some ammunition were found buried in the sand.[50]

Borderlands historians will be forever grateful to the two officers who took the time to sketch a diagram of the presidio. Although there was some deterioration, the walls were still standing and the buildings comparatively intact. Roscoe and Margaret Conkling included a copy of the diagram as Plate 50 in Volume 3 of *The Butterfield Overland Mail, 1857–1869*, and provided the following description of the presidio:

> The outside walls inclosed [sic] a tract approximately twelve hundred feet square, and so laid out that their angles corresponded to the four cardinal points. An inner walled inclosure [sic], rectangular in shape, contained the officers' quarters, barracks, a large chapel, a magazine and other buildings. The stables were in what might be termed the bailey between the inner and outer walls. Watch towers were attached to the inner walls. There were but two entrances into the inclosures [sic]. Both walls built of large adobes were over four feet in thickness and probably not less than eighteen feet in height. The buildings were all constructed of the same material. Altogether the presidio was a unique and impregnable fortress, and its preservation would have been of incalculable value historically.[51]

On 8 February 1847 Doniphan's army, together with 150 American merchants and 315 wagons of merchandise, departed El Paso del Norte for Chihuahua. At the Sacramento River, 15 miles north of the capital, the Mexicans made a stand. On 28 February they were completely routed, and Doniphan's army entered Chihuahua two days later. Feelings between Americans and Mexicans ran much higher than they had in El Paso del Norte, and the invading force destroyed far more property. According to Chihuahua historian Francisco Almada, Doniphan's men desecrated the cathedral, sacked some homes (including that of Governor Trías), seized the flour in the granary, cut the trees on the alameda for firewood, and destroyed part of an archive.[52]

As American forces occupied the various regions of the state, American merchants who had been held were released. James Magoffin, still regarded as an enemy alien, was an exception. He remained in custody in Durango until the end of the war, which came in September 1847 when General Winfield Scott's army captured Chapultepec Castle in Mexico City.[53]

Still, the machinery of Mexican government ground on. According to Article 5 of the Law of 16 December 1847, the states of Chihuahua, Coahuila, Nuevo León, Sonora, and Tamaulipas were "to complete, arm, and pay their respective presidial companies, which would be classed as national guards." More than a year later another law was passed that specifically abrogated Article 5. The presidial companies were to continue in place until such time as a "general plan for the defense and security of the frontier" could be established. The presidio of San Elizario, though now a ghost, still existed the minds of the bureaucrats in Mexico City long after the people of the community had begun to carry off the adobes of its formidable walls.[54]

SAN ELIZARIO, TEXAS, 1848–1900

FORTY-NINERS, MERCHANTS, SETTLERS, AND SOLDIERS, 1848–1850

FORTY-NINERS, MERCHANTS, SETTLERS, AND SOLDIERS, 1848-1850

The Treaty of Guadalupe Hidalgo, signed on 2 February 1848, officially ended the war between the United States and Mexico. The momentous territorial changes in the treaty reshaped a significant portion of the North American continent. It provided that the new international boundary between the United States and Mexico was to be "the Rio Grande . . . following the deepest channel . . . to the point where it strikes the southern boundary of New Mexico; thence, westwardly, along the whole southern boundary of New Mexico (which runs north of the town called Paso) to its western termination," north to the Gila River, then following the Gila until it empties into the Colorado River, and westward to the Pacific. Thus, all of the territory north of that line, known as the Mexican Cession and comprising a considerable portion of Mexico's national domain, became a part of the United States, which was to pay Mexico $15,000,000 in exchange.[1]

In late January 1848, less than two weeks before the signing of the treaty that gave the American Southwest to the United States, gold was discovered in California. Within a short time hordes of adventurers, opportunists, larger-than-life characters, discharged soldiers, outlaws, wife deserters, and debtors descended on the El Paso area. Among them was the first Anglo female resident, a six-foot Amazon known as "The Great Western," who possessed more than adequate physical endowments and was as generous with her affections as she was handy with a gun. Overnight the quiet little adobe town of El Paso del Norte was transformed into a bustling, brawling frontier crossroads, described as "the last place to rest, purchase supplies, ask directions, secure passports," and refresh dehydrated bodies with generous allotments of "Pass Whiskey."[2]

Contemporary sources report that by mid-1849 four thousand emigrants and twelve to fifteen hundred wagons were encamped north of the river across from El Paso del Norte. The price of mules, wagons, and provisions soared to such levels that the native Mexican population began to hoard provisions, causing strained relations between the emigrants and Mexicans and considerable disorder. Yet some of the new arrivals decided to remain in the area, so that by late 1849 Anglo-Americans had founded five settlements, roughly a mile or two apart, along the left bank of the Rio Grande. These were Frontera, established in 1848 by T. Frank White as a trading post; El Molino, the flour mill of Mexican War veteran Simeon Hart; the mercantile store of Benjamin Franklin Coons, located on the ranch purchased from Juan María Ponce de León, paseño aristocrat; Magoffinsville, east of Coons's property, where veteran Chihuahua merchant, James W. Magoffin, received visitors in the elegant manner; and the property of merchant-miner Hugh Stephenson, later called Concordia.[3]

In 1848 Colonel John M. Washington, the military governor of New Mexico, appointed T. Frank White of Frontera prefect and ordered him to declare his jurisdiction over all territory north and east of the river, formerly a part of Chihuahua. White removed local Mexican officials, made his own appointments, and warned Mexicans south of the river against trespassing on American territory. A local official filed a report of these events with his superior in San Elizario in January 1849.

At around three o'clock in the afternoon of 12 January, an individual whom Prefect White had commissioned appeared in San Elizario with a force of troops under the command of their own officer. Through an interpreter, the municipal president, Juan Pedro Pérez, received a message to appear in the *casas consistoriales*. No one was there when he arrived, and he received another message that White had summoned him to Nepomuceno Sambrano's house. When Pérez met with White, who immediately asked him for his credentials, Pérez produced them without delay. White calmly slipped them in his satchel.

Through the interpreter, White told Pérez that he no longer had any authority. Despite the fact that he did not agree with what he had been told, Pérez said,

Fine, I cannot oppose force, but this is an outrage or a dispossession, which I protest before God and man and their concurrence in the laws of my nation. Had my appointment been illegitimate under Mexican law, I would never cease to appeal any action that would besmirch my honor, just as I would with United States law.

White merely listened and then, in Pérez's presence, selected Santos Lucero justice of the peace. White then gave Lucero full authority to hear cases and decide what he thought was legal without having to commit anything to writing. In February the prefect of El Paso del Norte reported as a simple matter of fact that an armed force of the United States had occupied Ysleta, Socorro, and San Elizario and had taken possession of the ejidos and woods belonging to the three towns. In vain, Mexican officials, both state and local, continued to protest the seizures and the unilateral action taken by the United States in determining the boundary. By the end of 1849, eight settlements were located north of the river—the five White, Hart, Coons, Magoffin, and Stephenson had established, together with the three Mexican towns—Ysleta, Socorro, and San Elizario, which the shifting river had placed on the American side. A bilingual, bicultural, binational complex was taking shape at the historic "Pass of the North."[4]

By late 1848 there were a number of compelling reasons for establishing a United States military post on the Rio Grande—defense of the new boundary, protection of settlers against Apache attacks, and maintenance of law and order, needed now more than ever with the arrival of so many California emigrants. Secretary of War William L. Marcy's recommendation in July 1848 calling for the establishment of a post on the north side of the Rio Grande opposite El Paso del Norte was finally implemented with the arrival of six companies of infantry from San Antonio on 8 September 1849 under the command of Major Jefferson Van Horne. Two companies were stationed at San Elizario, and the other four were quartered across the river from El Paso del Norte on the ranch belonging to Benjamin F. Coons, known as the "Post Opposite El Paso."[5]

Nineteen-year-old Robert Eccleston, who arrived in El Paso with his friends in September 1849 while en route to California, left one of the most informative sketches of life in San Elizario in the gold-rush period. Young in years but mature in outlook, Eccleston recorded his impressions in a diary, a literary gem that has become an invaluable source of information about the Forty-Niners on the southwestern trail to California. Regarding San Elizario, he wrote:

> About 10 o'clock we entered Presidio, the first settlement after being for nearly 3 months out of the pale of civilization . . . . It was pleasant to see houses, even though they were made of mud. This town, I learn, contains 3 or 4000 inhabitants. The houses are built of mud & rough timber. The walls are not exactly plumb, but they are just as comfortable inside as if they were. The walls are about 10 ft. high & the houses contain but one story. Their fences are also made of mud, about four ft. high, & then taper to a point. The general appearance of the houses & fences is that of free stone, although the mud is hardly dark enough. The windows of the aristocracy are sometimes ornamented with carved wood grating, &c. Trees loaded with fruit might be seen in every garden, & baskets of the same at nearly every door. What I supposed to be the Catholic Church stood to the left of the road, having a steeple something like that of a castle. I did not alight as we passed through, it being my turn to stay near our wagon. I noticed a few handsome signorinas [sic] who were variously employed in carrying water in large earthen globes on their heads, or baskets of fruit, or picking fruit, &c.

> The old men & women were sitting at their doors with their eyes and ears wide open. The men dress generally in white domestic muslin. Their pants are tight around the thighs but wider as they hang down the leg. Their shirt or coat, whichever it may be called, is of the same stuff & made something like our shirts, having, however, wider sleeves & not being open at the side. Their hats are generally of different kind of straw with wide leafs. Those that can afford better clothes dress more like us having regular coats. The women dress much like Americans, generally having a scarf or handkerchief over their shoulders & heads. The skirts of their dresses seem to be separate from the body, & something of a different color, white, blue, &c. The smaller children are nearly naked.[6]

As to the establishment of a permanent site for the

military post in the area, both Van Horne and his commander at San Elizario, Captain William S. Henry, favored the old presidio. Van Horne believed it could be repaired and rebuilt at little expense. With a few adjacent buildings that could be rented or bought on moderate terms, he pointed out, the presidio could be made to quarter four or even six companies. Wood was plentiful, grazing was good, and the people, he said, were orderly and well behaved. Finally he pointed out that if troops were stationed at the old presidio, they would be removed from the wretched swarm of gamblers, drunkards, and desperadoes in El Paso del Norte.[7]

Captain Henry strongly urged that San Elizario be established as a permanent post, saying that "the Island" could produce grain enough to support all the troops in New Mexico. Furthermore, the presence of troops in San Elizario had given the residents a feeling of security for their lives and property, which in the past had been at the mercy of the Indians. He continued:

> I know of no better site for the garrison than that of the old presidio at present occupied by my command. It is a square of about 800 feet front and belongs to the Government. It is a perfect ruin from which I have been enabled to obtain shelter for the companies. The remaining portions of the old establishment are perfectly worthless, except for the immense number of "adobes" which could be saved and beneficially used for building purposes.

In the interior of the enclosure on the south face is a church and a small lot of ground for the padre, which is claimed by the people. The church I think will soon fall down. There is sufficient ground for all purposes to build a neat and pretty garrison for two companies.[8]

Captain Henry then went on to point out a number of additional advantages: ample ground for gardens, the availability of materials that could be used to fill up the present grounds and elevate the surface a few feet to provide drainage, the "admirable" soil for the manufacture of brick, and the existing irrigation ditches, which could provide an adequate supply of water. Moreover, there were enough adobes on hand to build another church for the people, as well as timbered land for a supply of wood. A portable grist mill could be brought in, he added, so that the companies could buy their own wheat and grind their own flour. Above all, he concluded, since the Indians were mounted, horses should be brought in, and all pistols should be revolvers, as they were the only arms adequate for the pursuit of Indians.[9]

In spite of Captain Henry's numerous arguments in favor of the old presidio, the military authorities ruled that its facilities were too limited to accommodate six companies as a permanent garrison. The two companies remained at the old presidio until 1851, when all troops were removed from the El Paso area. Meanwhile, the county of El Paso was established in March 1850 with San Elizario as the county seat. John Russell Bartlett, the boundary commissioner, visited the town in 1851 and found the presidio and church in a ruined condition. By that time the residents of the town had dismantled the presidial walls and damaged the other buildings in order to obtain adobes to construct or enlarge their own residences. In an effort to save at least some of the buildings, the Texas legislature passed an act on 13 December 1851 that deeded to the county of El Paso for its own purposes a tract of land where the old presidio and other buildings were located, but just how much was saved, of course, remains unknown—perhaps not much. Possibly the parishioners of San Elizario used some of the adobes to build a new church, completed in 1853.[10]

EL PASO COUNTY SEAT, 1850–1873

As hundreds of Anglo-Americans moved into the El Paso area in late 1849, complaints about the total absence of law and order became increasingly frequent and vociferous, and many began to look to the state of Texas as their only hope for relief. One of these was Rhode Island–born Charles A. Hoppin, who arrived in 1849 and established residence at San Elizario. Impressed with the beauty and potential of the Lower Valley, though greatly concerned about the conflicting and confusing political jurisdictions, Hoppin took the lead in appealing to Governor Peter H. Bell of Texas to extend the civil jurisdiction of the state and organize a county in the El Paso area. He wrote as follows from San Elizario on 3 January 1850:

> We are here, sir, situated in a beautiful valley containing from 1,000 to 1,500 inhabitants—the majority of whom are Mexicans, but Americans are daily coming in, and but a few years will elapse before this island will become an important point from its position, fertility of soil, & abundant production. It will teem with inhabitants—To whom does it belong? If to Texas, then, sir, Texas ought to give its citizens dwelling here the protection of her laws. Now we are in a region without law. It is true there is a prefect residing some miles above El Paso & there are in each of the small towns up on the island Alcaldes appointed by him. The Prefect received his appointment from the Governor of the Territory of New Mexico, but what laws govern the decisions of the Alcaldes I know not. I presume each one selects such a code as best suits him. Here the Alcalde, a very worthy Mexican, is governed by Laws enacted by the state of Chihuahua. We have no Magistrates, so clearly the situation in which we are placed tells me that I have a duty I owe to Law abiding citizens to present it to you. An American has been arrested and now is in the Guard House here charged with the revolting crime of rape. How can he be tried? If he is brought before an Alcalde has he the power of punishing if the charge is not proven? An American citizen is entitled to a jury trial. Who can summons the Jury? Who gives sentence? Who is authorized to execute the sentence if given? You see, sir, the necessity of organizing Courts for this part of the state. The people wish it and it is their right to ask it. If this is not a part of Texas, then from New Mexico they must ask the protection of Civil Laws. The organization of a county with the appointment of Magistrates and Judges would have a highly beneficial effect upon the population here. Let me ask you to confer upon me a great favor. I would be glad to receive a copy of the Laws of Texas. I do not think there is a copy this side of San Antonio, & important questions will arise requiring reference to the statutes. If you see fit to send it, direct it to the care of the "Officer Commanding, Post opposite El Paso."[11]

By the time Hoppin presented the case of the Anglo-American settlers, Texas had already decided to renew its old claim to everything east of the Rio Grande and make its bid for the El Paso area. In his message of 26 December 1849 Governor Bell called for the organization of western counties and the immediate extension of Texas's jurisdiction there, pointing out that many of the inhabitants had already made known their desire to be brought under the protection of the state. The legislature quickly responded, and on 31 December 1849 it designated new boundaries for Santa Fe County, reducing its size, while creating the three new counties of Presidio, El Paso, and Worth.[12]

On 3 January 1850 Governor Bell appointed Major Robert S. Neighbors commissioner to organize the counties and hold elections for county officers. Arriving in San Elizario in early February, Neighbors circulated a proclamation from Governor Bell explaining the history of Texas's claim to the region and calling upon all citizens to assist him in setting up the county. On 23 February Neighbors wrote Colonel John Munroe at Santa Fe of his arrival in the El Paso area for the purpose of extending the civil jurisdiction of Texas and announced his intention to visit Santa Fe after he had organized El Paso County. He added that he had encountered no opposition, had issued writs of election, and was proceeding to delimit the county, which extended from 60 miles below El Paso to 20 miles above the campsite of San Diego, and east to the Pecos River. Even after the Compromise of 1850 required Texas to yield its claim to New Mexico, the new county still encompassed 9,435 square miles.[13]

In elections held on 4 March 1850, 765 votes were cast for county officers. Charles A. Hoppin was elected chief justice of the county, a position later called county judge. Austin was the overwhelming choice for the state capital, and San Elizario, with its Mexican population of 1,200, became the seat of El Paso County. On 23 March 1850 Neighbors reported to Governor Bell that El Paso County was fully organized and that elected officials were discharging their duties.[14]

Hoppin served until 20 August 1850, when Connecticut-born Archibald C. Hyde replaced him. Establishing residence at San Elizario in the summer of 1850, he served two terms as county judge. His successor was Henry L. Dexter, one of the first Anglo-Americans to reside in Ysleta. In 1852–62 four Mexican-Americans were appoint-ed justices of the peace—Pedro Gonzales, Francisco Paso, Jesús Luján, and Juan Bautista Holguín; and six more became constables—Martín Durán, Julián Arias, Pedro Sisneros, Pedro Gonzales, Gregorio García, and Tomás Irigoyen. As district judge of the Eleventh Judicial District, the Texas legislature selected Joel L. Ankrim, a resident of San Elizario, who served from 1850 to 1856. His successor was Josiah Fraser Crosby, one of the great names in El Paso legal history, who served until 1861.[15]

Judging from Bartlett's description of a trial he observed in early 1851, a distinctly frontier style of justice prevailed. He wrote:

> It is doubtful whether in the whole history of trial by jury a more remarkable scene than the one here presented was ever exhibited. The trial took place in one of the adobe . . . houses peculiar to the country, which was dimly lighted from a single small window. Scarcely an individual was present who had not the appearance and garb of men who spend their lives on the frontier, far from civilization and its softening influences. Surrounded as we had been, and now were, by hostile Indians, and constantly mingling with half civilized and renegade men, it was necessary to go constantly armed. . . . In the court room, therefore, where one of the most solemn scenes of human experience was enacting, all were armed save the prisoners. There sat the judge, with a pistol lying on the table before him; the clerks and attorneys wore revolvers at their sides; and the jurors were either armed with similar weapons, or carried with them the unerring rifle. The members of the Commission and

citizens, who were either guarding the prisoners or protecting the court, carried by their sides a revolver, a rifle, or a fowling-piece, this presenting a scene more characteristic of feudal times than of the nineteenth century.[16]

During the 1850s the United States government inaugurated and conducted an extensive program of exploration in West Texas, one phase of a general policy of developing the entire trans-Mississippi country in the interest of the immigrant, the settler, the soldier, and the merchant. A significant aspect of the program was the exploration and survey of the most suitable routes for the construction of transcontinental railroads across the trans-Mississippi west to the Pacific Ocean. One of these was the southern route, extending from central Texas westward through the Pass of the North, then along the thirty-second parallel south of the Gila River to southern California. W. H. Emory, the United States boundary surveyor-commissioner, had noted in 1846 that the Sierra Madre and Rocky Mountains lost their continuous character at about the thirty-second parallel. "It is possible," he wrote,

> to pass through the mountain system, in this region, near the parallel of 32°, almost on the level of the plateau; so that if the sea were to rise 4,000 feet above its present level, the navigator could cross the continent near the 32d parallel of latitude. He would be on soundings of uniform depth, from the Gulf of California to the Pecos river. He would see to the north and to the south prominent peaks and sierras, and at times his pas-

sage would be narrow and intricate. At El Paso he would be within gun-shot of both shores.[17]

Possibly the most enthusiastic champion of the thirty-second parallel as the best for construction of a transcontinental railroad was Captain John Pope, who in 1854 conducted the most comprehensive survey of that line from the Rio Grande east to the Red River. His views became gospel for the merchants of the El Paso area such as Magoffin, Hart, and Stephenson, who never ceased to dream of a transcontinental railroad connecting East and West through El Paso.[18]

With the opening of two new, important wagon roads from San Antonio to the El Paso area in 1849 came the inauguration of mail service from San Antonio through San Elizario to Santa Fe, New Mexico. First to carry the mail was a big, broad-shouldered frontiersman named Henry Skillman, who signed a contract with the Post Office Department in late 1850 and initiated a monthly passenger service using four-horse coaches. The fare from San Antonio to the El Paso area was fixed at $100 and through fare to Santa Fe at $125. Passengers were allowed 40 pounds of baggage. Joining Skillman as stage driver was another frontier character, the fabled William Alexander Wallace, nicknamed "Bigfoot" for his longstanding feud with a Lipan Apache who left huge moccasin tracks in his path. The purchase of new, improved carbines produced by the Sharps Rifle Manufacturing Company gave the drivers and guards a needed and welcome advantage in dealing with the Apaches. By early 1853 the entire trip from Santa Fe to San Antonio could be completed in twenty-four days, with only sixteen of them comprising the El Paso-San Antonio leg.[19]

The increased volume of mail necessitated the establishment of a post office in 1852 for El Paso, Texas. The name Franklin, however (spelled Franquilín in the Mexican documents), continued to be used by officials on both sides of the border for a number of years, probably to avoid confusion with the name El Paso del Norte. The first postmaster was Jarvis Hubbell, appointed in July 1852, followed by A. C. Hyde in March 1855 and Ben Dowell in March 1857. Skillman continued his service until 1854, when he lost his federal subsidy, and all efforts during the next three years to keep the line going failed. George H. Giddings finally obtained a contract to establish a semi-monthly mail service between San Antonio and San Diego, California, in 1857 and began a mail and passenger service the following May. Often called the "Jackass Line" because of its use of mules over most of the route, the service left from both ends twice a month; the fare was $200, with a baggage allowance of 30 pounds. Eighty-seven stage stations, most of them merely mud huts, were erected, and the run became known as "the longest uninterrupted route in the United States," if not in the world. There were two stations located in the El Paso area—one in San Elizario owned by Hyde and William (Bill) Ford, and the other in Franklin owned by Dowell. Each had a grocery store, rooms, billiard parlor, and saloon, and was a most popular gathering place.[20]

Another means of transportation tested in the Southwest before the Civil War was the use of camels as beasts of burden. The experiment should come as no surprise when one recalls that the West in the textbooks of the period was labeled "The Great American Desert." Although the idea had been advanced on a number of occasions, it failed to gain acceptance until 1854. At that time Lieutenant Edward Fitzgerald Beale, a veteran of the Mexican War who thought camels might prove useful in the Southwest, found support from Jefferson Davis, secretary of war in the Franklin Pierce administration. Necessary funds were appropriated, and by February 1857 77 animals had been imported and stabled at a camp 60 miles northwest of San Antonio. In late June 1857 a wagon train and a caravan of 25 camels, each carrying about 500 pounds, left camp. Commanded by Lieutenant Beale, they arrived in San Elizario on 26 July. The wagon train continued on through the town, but the camels were detained in San Elizario for all to see. "Our train arrived this morning of July 26," wrote Lieutenant Beale,

> and the whole Mexican population, which since our arrival had been in a perfectly feverish state of excitement in relation to the camels, had their curiosity gratified. The street was

crowded, and when we went on to camp the whole town followed. I drove to Franklin in the evening, and spent the next day at Fort Bliss, where I was kindly received by the officers. I dined with Mr. MacGoffin [sic] and attended a pleasant party at his house afterwards.[21]

In 1856–57 John C. Reid of Selma, Alabama, and his three friends spent ten months on a "tramp" of the American Southwest. In the El Paso area he was impressed with the productivity of the valleys; of the Lower Valley settlements he liked San Elizario best. He preferred Magoffinsville to Stephenson's Ranch and thought the facilities and strong adobe structures at Fort Bliss displayed good planning. Most impressive was the town of Franklin, said Reid, with its half-dozen dry goods stores, customhouse, and post office. With the completion of an inter-oceanic railroad, he predicted, it would occupy an important midway position and could become the most important inland city in America.

While there was much in El Paso del Norte that he liked—the fandangos, the fiesta of Our Lady of Guadalupe, the friendliness of the people, and the beautiful ladies—there was much he found distasteful—poverty, peonage, deteriorated buildings, the tariff, beggars, and thieves. On the whole, however, Reid was highly impressed with the El Paso area and remained fully convinced that the thirty-second parallel offered far more advantages for a transcontinental railroad than any of the other possible routes. The South, he insisted, must shake off its lethargy, assert itself in defense of its interests, and build "that commercial empire which is ours by manifest and inevitable destiny." Published in 1858, *Reid's Tramp*, with its persuasive arguments in support of a southern transcontinental railroad, provided the El Paso leadership in 1860–61 with a rationale for casting its lot with the Confederacy.[22]

In September 1858 a new transportation service established between St. Louis and San Francisco exerted a far greater impact on the El Paso area than any other until the arrival of the railroad. This was John Butterfield's Overland Mail, a company that had contracted a year earlier to carry mail and passengers by stage from Tipton, Missouri, where the railroad terminated, to San Francisco, completing the entire trip in no more than twenty-five days. The Butterfield system would span the longest distance over which coach service had ever been attempted, involving 2,700 miles of mud, dust, and rock-covered trail. Granted the difficulties were enormous, but John Butterfield's experience and determination proved equal to the task. Each stage, pulled by four or six horses or mules, could carry six to eight passengers in addition to the mail. Stations were constructed on average about twenty miles apart; there passengers could get water and a simple meal while a fresh team of horses or mules was hitched to the coach. Baggage allowance was 40 pounds; fare for the entire distance was $200; sleep and relaxation were not guaranteed.[23]

The little community of Franklin made impressive strides in the period from 1858 to 1861. Anson Mills, one of El Paso's foremost pioneers, arrived in May 1858. He brought with him a background in surveying (which he had received at West Point) and a conviction that the El Paso area was a land of promise that would eventually become a place of importance. The Butterfield company contracted him to design and construct its station. Completed in September 1858, about the time the first stage arrived, the building and corrals were constructed on two acres bounded by Oregon, Overland, and El Paso Streets, making the station the largest and best equipped on the Butterfield route. Occupying half a city block, it was the most imposing structure in town. Across the street where the Camino Real Paso del Norte Hotel now stands was Ben Dowell's post office, store, and saloon—the favorite meeting place in town.[24]

Early in 1859 Mills completed his survey and plat of the town of El Paso with its public square (now San Jacinto Plaza), small plaza with a bulletin board nailed to a tree, and the principal streets named for the stage lines. According to the 1860 census the population was 428, and the outlook was bright.

The Civil War and Reconstruction, however, stunted growth and development for more than a decade. "From the first I foresaw the prospective importance of the place," noted William Wallace Mills, who had arrived in December 1858, some six months after his elder brother, Anson,

> and many a still, lonesome night have I listened to the roaring of the waters over the dam at Harts Mill, a mile above the village, and tried to fancy it the rumbling of railroad trains, which were then fifteen hundred miles away. No, I do not claim to have foreseen that El Paso would be the center of so many railroads, but I felt sure that the first road to the Pacific Ocean would pass through El Paso, and *so it would*, had it not been for the Rebellion.[25]

News of the election of Abraham Lincoln in 1860, the candidate of the party opposing the extension of slavery into the territories of the United States, brought forth immediate action on the part of the Southern states, including Texas. Even before Lincoln's inaugural on 4 March 1861, seven Southern states had held conventions that adopted ordinances of secession from the Union. On 1 February 1861 a state convention in Austin voted overwhelmingly in favor of secession. In El Paso the American population, comprising the vast majority, showed only limited interest, but the Anglo-Americans were almost unanimously pro-South. Although a few, such as Simeon Hart, owned slaves, the issue of slavery locally was hardly the burning issue it had become nationally. A more significant explanation for the overwhelming pro-South sentiment was the identification of Jefferson Davis, president of the Confederate States, with the southern transcontinental railroad route and its obvious implications for El Paso's future.

On receipt of the news of the action of the state convention, a local election on the question of Texas's secession was held in Ben Dowell's saloon. Two opposition votes were cast, and everyone in town knew whose they were—the Mills brothers, Anson and W. W. "Champagne for the secessionists!" shouted Simeon Hart when he saw W. W. Mills enter the saloon, "the noose for all Unionists!" Although the Mills brothers charged that the election was a fraud, since the nine hundred votes cast included several hundred by Mexicans from El Paso del Norte, there was little doubt of the decisive influence of the pro-Southerners such as Simeon Hart, James Magoffin, and Josiah Crosby.[27]

During the first year of the war, Confederate forces under Lieutenant Colonel John R. Baylor brought the El Paso area and southern New Mexico under control. James Magoffin ran up the Confederate flag at Fort Bliss, and the Mills brothers left the area. Captain Bethel Coopwood organized the San Elizario Spy Company, which consisted of two hundred long-eared, ragged Texans—"backwoodsmen, ranchers and cowboys who knew the country from San Antonio to Santa Fe, New Mexico, and from mountain to mountain on both sides of the Rio Grande" — most of them Indian fighters. They captured two hundred horses and mules at the federal garrison at Fort Fillmore, along with the Seventh United States Infantry at Mesilla, and twelve army supply wagons at Cañada Alamosa. For the remainder of 1861 they held the Mesilla Valley.[28]

Confederate forces under the command of General Henry H. Sibley occupied Albuquerque and Santa Fe, but suffered terrible losses at Glorieta Pass, Pigeon's Point, and Apache Canyon. In June 1862 the California Column brought Arizona and New Mexico under Union control, and Magoffin left for San Antonio, while others fled across the river. Later that year the town of Zaragoza, Chihuahua, was founded, named for the hero of the Battle of Puebla on 5 May 1862. It was settled by Mexicans from the Lower Valley and some Tiguas from Ysleta who were discontented with the rule of American officials.[29]

In the United States, the Civil War was followed by a period equally as bitter and painful: Reconstruction. With the South in ruins and the Democratic party splintered and broken, the leadership of the Republican party remained unchallenged for a decade or more. Significant change occurred in the political leadership in El Paso as many of those who had served as officers and soldiers with the California Column, such as Albert H. French, James A. Zabriskie, and Albert J. Fountain, took over positions of leadership, power, and influence. This new group looked to W. W. Mills, who had returned to El Paso, served as collector of customs from 1863 to 1869, and became the principal organizer of the local Republican party. With assistance from French and Zabriskie, Mills formed the "customhouse ring," a vehicle for giving favors to local merchants, controlling appointments to office, and manipulating elections. During the late sixties and early seventies, it was rare indeed in El Paso when a local election was not characterized by fraud, vote purchasing, ballot stuffing, bribery, intimidation, or tampering by corrupt election officials.[30]

The Mexican population in Ysleta found the new Republican leadership under Mills to be oppressive and complained to Governor J. W. Throckmorton. "We were forcibly seized and kidnapped by one French," the petition began,

> and we were imprisoned and afterwards sent into the town of El Paso del Norte, Mexico, where, without being informed of the offense or the charges against us, we were immediately thrown into jail. . . . We have been separated from our businesses and families, a particularly cruel treatment, since we are small farmers and poor, dependent upon our daily labor for our support. No comforts or food are allowed us unless from our own homes some twelve or fifteen miles distant. . . . We are not the first who have suffered in the same way within the last three years, and unless some remedy is found for this gross injustice and growing evil, we will not be the last victims of oppression and tyranny supported by bayonets, where none

save martial law is respected and anarchy reigns supreme, although on Texas soil.[31]

The "List of Registered Voters" in El Paso compiled from 1867 to 1869 indicates a total of 741 in the county's four precincts. Of these, all but 82 were Mexican-Americans, most of whom were illiterate and cast their votes by making a mark. Of the 82, 11 had come from Europe, 2 were designated "colored," and the rest were from the United States, particularly New England and the Middle West. Of the 69 from the United States only 19 had been in the El Paso area for three years or more. On the other hand, 145 Mexican-American voters had lived in the Lower Valley for forty years or longer.[32]

Quick to perceive the importance of the Mexican-American vote, the Mills group soon found ways to co-opt it. It was necessary to speak and conduct county business in Spanish, establish alliances with key Mexican-American leaders, and elect a few to county office. In his capacity as U.S. collector of customs at El Paso, Mills brought together a coalition of Mexican-Americans led by Luis Cardis, an Italian-born stagecoach manager, and Father Antonio Borrajo, the fiery Catholic priest of San Elizario. The coalition easily won the elections of 1866. Mexican-Americans elected in this Republican victory included J. M. Luján, county clerk; Máximo Aranda, district clerk; and justices of the peace José María González, Julián Arias, and Gregorio N. García.[33]

By 1867 the Republican party had come under the control of the radical wing, which called for an ironclad oath to the United States Constitution for officeholders. The party program supported black suffrage; disfranchisement of former Confederates; ratification of the Thirteenth (abolishing slavery), the Fourteenth (making blacks citizens of the United States), and the Fifteenth (giving blacks the vote) Amendments; and military rule to ensure these objectives. In El Paso, W. W. Mills was named delegate to a constitutional convention in June 1868 in Austin, where the radical majority selected Edmund J. Davis as president. A. J. Hamilton, Mills's father in law, led those in opposition who favored a more moderate policy on Reconstruction. President Andrew Johnson had appointed Hamilton provisional governor, but Throckmorton defeated him in the gubernatorial election of 1866. Although Mills had maintained a neutral position on Reconstruction in El Paso, he increasingly gave his support to his father-in-law's moderate views.[34]

During Mills's year in Austin, El Paso Republican party leadership fell to A. J. Fountain, who, unlike Mills, gave his full support to the radical Republican program. By early 1869 it was clear that Mills and Fountain were heading for a showdown. Moderate Republicans in their convention in Austin nominated Hamilton for governor and Mills for legislative representative from El Paso. A radical convention in Corpus Christi then nominated Edmund J. Davis for governor and Fountain for El Paso representative. Davis's influence with the national Republican party leaders was decisive, and Mills was removed from his post as collector of customs, thus sharply curtailing his local power and influence.[35]

For as long as anyone could remember, the Mexican population in the Lower Valley had gathered salt, which was free for the taking, from the Guadalupe salt beds, located one hundred miles east of El Paso. Word had leaked out, however, that Mills and a group had attempted to secure title in order to collect a fee for extracted salt and that they had rejected Fountain's suggestion to abandon the enterprise. Although the title obtained by the Mills group was found defective and the salt beds remained public land, Fountain cleverly exploited the issue politically by attacking Mills for attempting to appropriate from the Mexican-Americans what he claimed was rightfully theirs.[36]

The confrontation between Mills and Fountain took place in San Elizario on 30 November during the election for a seat in the Texas legislature. It lasted for four days, with a detachment of soldiers checking credentials and counting the ballots. Although there were only 122 registered voters in the county, 273 votes were cast in the election. Mills claimed that he won by 95 votes, but the returns showed that he lost by 139 votes. He declared that the election judges had scratched out his name on 143 ballots and written in Fountain's. Since the Davis radical Republicans swept all state offices, however, Fountain was declared elected over the once-powerful Mills.[37]

By 1872 radical Republican rule had run its course with the defeat of Governor Edmund J. Davis. In El Paso the need for a major political realignment had become all too evident to Charles Howard, a strong-willed Democrat and shrewd politician. He wasted no time in enlisting the support of Cardis, whose polished Spanish brought him a large following from the Mexican-American population. Moreover, Cardis had a staunch ally in Father Borrajo, who threatened to excommunicate any Catholic who voted the Republican ticket.[38]

Early in 1873 Howard and Cardis confidently concluded that the political breezes were beginning to blow their way. They drew up a petition to the Texas legislature, dated 19 February 1873, which carried more than 350 signatures, mostly those of Mexicans, with many written in the same hand. "For more than three years," it began,

> the voice of the legal voters of this county has been suppressed by fraud on the part of those whose duty it was under the law to see that all elections were fairly conducted—we have been misrepresented and calumniated by men who have thrust themselves into office against our wishes and consent, most of whom were strangers to us, and who by their oppressive, insolent, and arbitrary conduct in office have forfeited all claims to our confidence and respect. . . . These frauds of the past three years were in a great measure planned and executed through

> the instrumentality of A. J. Fountain, at present a member of Your Honorable Body, into which he crept by a fraud and trick perpetrated by him as our representative, and we declare him a disgrace to our county and a blemish upon Your Honorable Body.

The petition then focused on Simon Bolivar Newcomb, district judge of El Paso County. "He was appointed by the influence of A. J. Fountain," it stated,

> and has ever since been his willing and superserviceable tool, and he has prostituted his office to the obtaining of partisan ends, and has brought odium and contempt upon his court. . . .We believe that he renders his judgments through favoritism and for money, and that he has leagued himself with our enemies and oppressors. We therefore most earnestly beg of Your Honorable Body that he may be removed from his position, and that some capable and honest man be placed in his stead.

Finally the petition declared that the electorate of El Paso County had been cheated of their votes in the elections of 1869; ballots were changed in the ballot box, and officers who had been defeated by a large majority were declared elected by the Fountain faction.[39]

The seat of El Paso County, established in San Elizario in 1850, was moved to Ysleta on 18 February 1867, but was returned to San Elizario on 31 August 1868. Here it remained until 1873 when the Texas legislature ordered an election to determine its future location. In the balloting on 7 December 1873, the county seat was moved from

San Elizario back to Ysleta by a vote of 259 to 222, even though San Elizario, with a population of 1,120 had 300 more residents than Ysleta. In the twenty-three-year period that the county seat had been in San Elizario, Anglo-Americans had held most of the county offices in the 1850s, but during the 1860s a group of dedicated Mexican-Americans began to play a much greater role in county affairs. In the meantime, in May 1873 El Paso, with a population of about 800, was incorporated as a town, so from this time forward the political center of gravity shifted to the El Paso-Ysleta area.[40]

MEXICAN-AMERICAN LEADERSHIP IN THE 1860S AND 1870S

The town of San Elizario in the period following the Civil War was virtually unchanged from its presidio days. It had remained a community of farmworkers, with a population of slightly more than a thousand. The two-room adobe structure remained the general pattern for almost all residences, with poverty and illiteracy as widespread as ever. Here were the vineyards, the wheat and corn fields, the ejidos, and the life-giving acequia. The presidio and its chapel were in ruins, as the residents by 1851 had dismantled the walls of the buildings, using the adobes to construct or enlarge their living quarters and build high walls around them for protection against the Apaches. Presumably the presidio's adobes were used to build a small church, completed in 1853. All the land in the town of San Elizario, with the exception of a few privately owned parcels, was held in common for the benefit of all inhabitants. Here in this impoverished community, beginning in the 1850s, there emerged a small group of dedicated, self-educated farm owners who displayed vigorous leadership and deep concern for the welfare of the community and its people. One of these was Gregorio N. García.[41]

Gregorio García was born to a San Elizario presidial couple in 1819, the last years of the Spanish period. Mexican independence presented a new situation for military personnel, but since almost all had been born and raised in territory that became the new nation of Mexico, they presumably had little difficulty in shifting their allegiance and accepting the new order under the Mexican flag. At the age of fourteen, García joined the Mexican army. He taught himself how to read and write and had become the owner of a house and farm by the time he was nineteen. In 1841 he married María de los Santos Albillar. Hearing of the Texas revolution and possible plans for the Texas invasion of New Mexico, García contributed a peso to a fund-raising campaign to resist the Texans. He fought in the Mexican War and during the 1850s served in the new county government as justice of the peace and

county commissioner. In the late 1850s he built a house for his family on the plaza, the largest and most impressive structure in town. Officially named Casa García, it has become better known as Los Portales, because of its architectural features. In time it served as a meeting place for county officials, and in the 1870s it was converted into a school.[42]

García reached his political maturity in San Elizario in the 1860s while the W. W. Mills regime held sway in El Paso. The United States census of 1860 recorded that he and his wife, María, had six children with real and personal estates amounting to $5,600. Serving as justice of the peace from 1864 to 1870 with the assistance of a constable, García handled a large number of civil and criminal cases. His priorities during those years were the care and cleaning of the acequia, protection of timber resources, and improvement of working conditions. In the meantime there was a renewal of Apache hostilities in the area that gave him great concern.[43]

During the Civil War the United States government established a colony of Navajos and Mescalero Apaches at Bosque Redondo on the Pecos River in New Mexico. Hopes were high for its success, but ill luck dogged the project from the beginning. For one thing, it had been a serious mistake to include both Navajos and Mescalero Apaches, for they could not get along and were constantly fighting. Moreover, starvation, mismanagement, and even corruption became so scandalous that nine hundred Apaches and Navajos left the camp in 1864. The Santa Fe *New Mexican* decried the conditions prevailing at Bosque Redondo and revealed that cheating officials had squandered congressional appropriations. Their endurance at an end, the Mescaleros departed on the night of 3 November 1865. In no time they were back on the warpath, raiding the settlements of West Texas and the merchant caravans on the San Antonio-El Paso trail.[44]

Gregorio García immediately voiced his concern about renewed Apache hostilities. In a report to state officials he indicated that from August 1865 to February 1867 the Apaches had seized more than nine hundred sheep and goats; fourteen men had been killed near San Elizario during February and March 1866, victims of Apache raids. They prevented Máximo Aranda, who had been elected to the legislature, from attending the sessions in Austin. In 1871 García organized a hard-hitting frontier company and was named captain of the Santa Fe Force, which battled the Apaches for three years. Some gave up the warpath with the establishment of the Mescalero Apache Reservation in 1873, but not all. Captain García returned to San Elizario with an arrow wound in his arm, which paralyzed it for the rest of his life. By that time, his reputation as San Elizario's greatest Indian fighter had been well established. Teléforo Montes, who had replaced García as justice of the peace in 1871, now replaced him in the field. With a company of Texas Rangers, Montes battled the Apaches for the next two years.[45]

On 5 April 1871 the Texas legislature passed an act incorporating the town of San Elizario; its boundaries were those described in a patent in 1853. The 1871 act gave the town council of San Elizario the authority to grant or sell portions of the town's property to its citizens. For many years, however, no council seems to have been elected, and the land was held in common as before. Municipal records indicate that the town had a mayor, J. Mauro Luján, in 1875, but the status of its incorporation during that time is not entirely clear. A formal incorporation of the town (or second incorporation), according to new legislation passed in 1879, took place on 9 February 1880.[46]

In 1877 the peace and tranquility of the Rio Grande Valley came to an abrupt halt with the outbreak of the bloodiest civil disorder in the county's history. Known as the Salt War, it contained all the ingredients of a violent and vicious border dispute, setting Anglo-American against Mexican-American, strong man against strong man, faction against faction, and the United States against Mexico. Bad blood, personal rivalries, and racial hostilities characterized the ugly affair. Most of the resulting mob violence, rape, looting, and murder took place in and around San Elizario, the former county seat and at that time still the largest settlement in the county.[47]

The Salt War began as a personal struggle between former allies, Judge Charles Howard and Luis Cardis, the Italian immigrant who had won a seat in the Texas legislature. When Howard announced that the hundreds of acres of salt beds east of El Paso were now his private property and that a fee would be charged for salt, Cardis saw an opportunity to champion Mexican interests and increase his own political following. Raising his voice in protest to Howard's action, Cardis found support among the Mexican population of San Elizario and a valuable ally in Father Borrajo, the parish priest. Several fistfights occurred between the two antagonists before Howard, armed with a shotgun, found Cardis in Solomon Schutz's store on San Francisco Street in El Paso on 10 October 1877 and killed him with a blast to his chest.[48]

News of the killing spread like wildfire. Captain Gregorio García became county judge at a time when all law in the valley had broken down. At Ysleta a meeting was called to discuss ways and means of getting rid of the county judge, who continued to support his law-and-order stance. Some were for killing him at once to save trouble, whereupon Martín Alderete rose to remind them that they were American citizens. At once the assembly was on its feet shouting, "No, we are Mexicans till we die! — ¡Hasta la muerte, hasta la muerte!"[49]

It was just a matter of time before a group of Mexicans from both sides of the river captured Howard in San Elizario. There a firing squad cut him down. Two of Howard's bondsmen were killed and their personal effects taken to Mexico. The homes of Howard's supporters were pillaged. An untrained group of Texas Rangers was forced to surrender after two of their number were killed. Fort Bliss was closed at the time for lack of funds, and on both sides of the border there was talk of war between the United States and Mexico. Before a semblance of order was finally restored, a posse of thirty volunteers from Silver City, New Mexico, had ravaged the Lower Valley towns, killing residents and destroying property. A congressional investigation early in 1878 collected evidence, but no one was arrested, tried, or convicted. Fort Bliss was reestablished in El Paso, and in time the Mexican families of the Lower Valley were allowed to haul salt for a fee under the watchful eye of a Texas Ranger.[50]

In early February 1878, about a month after the bloody Salt War, there arrived in San Elizario a young man of eighteen years, impressive looks and bearing, with a command of English and Spanish—obviously the product of careful training and an exceptional education. His name was Octaviano Larrazolo. At the age of ten in the small town of Valle de Allende, Chihuahua, he had caught the eye of John B. Salpointe, bishop of Arizona. After appropriate arrangements were made with the family regarding the bishop's responsibility for the boy's education and development, he received schooling in Tucson, Las Cruces, and St. Michael's in Santa Fe. Excelling in public speaking, the young scholar had an outstanding record and completed his formal education in 1876 at the age of seventeen. Bishop Salpointe then escorted young Larrazolo to the parishes of Las Cruces, Ysleta, and San Elizario. Upon his arrival at San Elizario he visited with Peter Bourgade, the parish priest, and Gregorio N. García, Jr., a close friend, and informed them that he was seeking employment as a teacher. On 23 February 1878, by order of County Judge García, Larrazolo was employed at the San Elizario Public School. His contract stipulated a salary of two dollars per pupil, so long as it did not exceed fifty dollars a month. Casa García became a school overnight. The following year his parents and three siblings moved to San Elizario; when his parents returned to Juárez, they left their other children with Octaviano. The United States census of 1880 identified Larrazolo as a schoolteacher, and all of the children of the town between the ages of six to twelve were listed "at school." The Mexican-American leadership of San Elizario and the young teacher from Chihuahua had made a significant beginning.[51]

The Garcías, father and son, furthered their involvement in town affairs when they hired A. Q. Wingo to survey the San Elizario grant in 1879. An earlier survey had been made in 1853, and a patent based on it had been approved and forwarded to the town of San Elizario. Community leaders must have considered the town to be unincorporated at this time, and therefore lacking the authority to allot occupied tracts to its residents. Thus the land continued to be held in common for the benefit of all the inhabitants. An act of the legislature in 1871 authorized the town to grant or sell portions of its property to citizens, but nothing was done until 1879. At that time the Garcías decided that an up-to-date survey of the San Elizario grant was necessary before the allotments could be made. Wingo completed the survey in October 1879, indicating that the San Elizario grant contained 40,869 acres.[52]

In the same year, 1879, the Sisters of Loretto opened St. Joseph's Academy in San Elizario, at a convent that had originally been a private residence. Wooden floors replaced earthen ones, and other buildings were gradually added. The reputation of the school soon attracted pupils from the valley, El Paso, and the interior of Mexico. Plans for a high school had begun when the grade school was moved to El Paso in 1892.[53]

OLD SAN ELIZARIO, 1880–1900

In February 1880 the town of San Elizario incorporated again, this time under the state's general incorporation laws, and was granted a special charter. Local ordinances provided for a mayor and town council of five *regidores*, or aldermen; a marshal; an *alcalde mayor de aguas*; and additional alcaldes as needed. The ordinances covered civil and criminal cases, the acequia, the plaza, the jail, the public school, private property, and unpenned livestock. They also provided for fines and penalties for violations and the assessment of fees for use of the acequia. All applications and petitions would receive due consideration. Should the town inhabitants wish to abolish a corporation, at least fifty voters would have to petition the county judge for an election, which would require a majority vote to effect the change.[54]

In January 1881 the town council of San Elizario, in the interest of securing a railway depot in the center of the community, offered the Texas and Pacific Railway Company a right-of-way one hundred feet wide through the middle of town. This generated so much opposition from the residents, however, that the Texas and Pacific chose to bypass San Elizario. The council then offered a right-of-way to the Galveston, Harrisburg and San Antonio through the town's corporate boundaries. By this time El Paso had obtained the Southern Pacific, its link with the Texas and Pacific, thus establishing the transcontinental railroad that Magoffin and other pioneers had envisioned.[55]

With the approach of the Texas and Pacific railroad being constructed nearby, the residents of the town, anticipating an increase in land values, demanded a distribution of all the lands being used and occupied. Six hundred and sixty-eight separate tracts located in the San Elizario grant were surveyed and conveyed to the inhabitants. Since many of these deeds were not executed on the form or with the formalities prescribed in the town's charter, the legislature passed a special act on 2 April 1889 that validated them. In addition, since San Elizario had incorporated under the state's general incorporation laws rather than the 1871 act, all was remedied by a special act passed on 17 March 1891. Within a year or so most farmworkers in San Elizario could claim ownership of a piece of land, a most significant development in the history of the town.[56]

The first mayor of San Elizario was Gregorio N. García, Jr., the son of the town's great leader, Captain Gregorio García. He was born in 1855, educated by his parents, and in 1874 married Romana Sánchez. Twenty-two years of age at the time of the Salt War when he was serving as justice of the peace, he joined his father, the county judge, in support of the law enforcement bodies. His administration passed San Elizario's first property tax in 1882, providing for an ad valorem tax of one-fourth of one percent on all property, both real and personal. His administration also sponsored an ordinance giving the mayor a dollar a day and the regidores fifty cents a day for their services. In a boundary dispute with Socorro that involved rich timber resources, Socorro was awarded 500 varas (at 33 inches to the vara) in 1883. The mayor's older brother, Tomás, succeeded him in office that same year.[57]

Gregorio García's good friend and associate, Octaviano Larrazolo, had continued his teaching and farming. In 1881 he married Rosalía Cobos, and two years later their first child was born. Following the death of his father in 1882, Larrazolo's mother had joined his household. His teaching salary was raised to seventy-five dollars, and he began serving the town council as secretary. On his recommendation, the council approved an ordinance establishing a free public school for girls, and Sister Margaret Mary of the Sisters of Loretto was employed as

teacher.[58]

By 1885 Larrazolo was supporting his growing family and his parents, who had moved to the border. He began to study law and became a citizen of the United States. Larrazolo then left the teaching profession, served as a court clerk of both the U.S. county circuit and district courts for El Paso, and was admitted to the bar in Texas. In 1886 he resigned his positions to run for district court, was elected and ran again in 1888. Larrazolo was elected district attorney for the Thirty-fourth Judicial District in 1889 and was reelected in 1892. His wife had died in childbirth in 1891, and in 1892 he married María García. She was the daughter of Carlos García, the niece of Gregorio N. García, Jr., and the valedictorian of her class at Loretto Academy, the last to graduate from San Elizario. Larrazolo worked briefly for a law firm in El Paso, but in 1895 he and María moved their family to New Mexico, which became their permanent home. In time Larrazolo served New Mexico as both governor and senator. His contribution to the development of San Elizario has never been forgotten.[59]

For more than a hundred years the most impressive structure in San Elizario has been the church, completed in 1887 after ten years' effort. The parish priest, Father Bourgade, and his successor, Father Andrew Echallier, supervised its construction. The main body of the building at that time had a triangular tower with a bell in the center and buttresses on the front and side walls. The interior had simple beams and posts. A fire that destroyed the sacristy in 1935 made necessary the complete restoration of the interior. Now in addition to the three aisles leading to the altar, there are elaborate wall decorations, and statuary adorns the entire interior.

> The Iglesia de San Elceario is an outstanding example of late adobe church architecture in the West Texas and New Mexico tradition. It reflects the influence of the European architectural styles on the earlier, simpler, box-like missions of the region. The plastered adobe walls and strong buttresses catch the southwestern sunlight at its best, as all adobe structures tend to do.[60]

During the nineteenth century, agriculture remained the dominant economic activity in the El Paso valley. Of the many visitors who were impressed with the area's abundance, the most enthusiastic champion of the area, its products, and its potential, was William M. Pierson, vice-consul of the United States in El Paso del Norte during the 1870s. The country was beautiful but isolated, wrote Pierson, the climate salubrious but arid, and the sandy soil intermixed with black loam. Timber was insufficient for farming demands, but "mud walls" dried in the sun made excellent and durable fences. Limited rainfall made irrigation absolutely necessary. On the American side of the valley, Pierson explained, about 15 square miles were being cultivated, mostly farmed by Mexicans, while on the Mexican side there was a solid mass under cultivation stretching downriver for 16 miles and varying in width from 6 to 10 miles. This, he added, represented only one fiftieth of the potential. The quality of the cereals produced, especially wheat, was excellent, as was that of the vegetables, particularly onions, which often reached three to four pounds in weight. Grapes and other fruits far surpassed those grown in the United States, and competent experts had judged area wines to be of the first rank among those made in North America. The wine yield of a healthy vineyard, said Pierson, was 250 gallons to the acre, and sold for one dollar a gallon. Grains, fruits, vegetables, and livestock were exported to Fort Bliss, but most of the wine was consumed in Mexico.[61]

For two centuries the lifeblood of the El Paso valley was its irrigation system. Dams were built to divert water from the Rio Grande into ditches averaging about four feet in depth and five feet in width, each community in the valley being fed by a diversion dam and ditch. Later, however, an *acequia madre*, or main ditch, was constructed that connected the various towns to a diversion dam built a short distance north of El Paso del Norte. During the Mexican period Juan María Ponce de León of El Paso del Norte built the first acequia north of the river on his property by placing a gate on the diversion dam.[62]

In 1848 the Rio Grande became the boundary between the United States and Mexico, which put Ponce's property and the Lower Valley settlements of Ysleta, Socorro, and San Elizario on the American side. James Magoffin extended "Ponce's Ditch," known as the Fort Bliss-Magoffinsville Acequia, and the Lower Valley settlements continued to draw water directly from the river. Then, during the 1850s, the town leaders of Franklin built a second dam just north of the other one (with a gate for each country), resulting in the construction of the El Paso Acequia. Once again, the Lower Valley settlements continued to draw from the river, if and when any water was available. With the incorporation of El Paso in 1873, which included Magoffinsville, one of the first acts of the new city administration was to pass ordinances regulating the use and maintenance of the acequias within city limits. Alice White, in her pioneer study, has written:

> As time went on the water situation in the valley became steadily more complex and alarming. Not only was a greater amount of water being taken from the river in Colorado and New Mexico but a much heavier demand was being made locally. The population was growing rapidly on both sides of the river and soon there developed a rivalry for the use of the river water not only between the Mexicans and the Americans on opposite sides of the Rio Grande, but also between the several communities on the American side.[63]

In 1881 the long-awaited railroad arrived in El Paso, ushering in a new era, and within a year El Paso's population equaled that of Ysleta, the county seat. This generated a movement by El Paso's civic leaders to move the county seat to El Paso. The citizens of Ysleta, confident that they had a better chance in 1883 of keeping the county seat than by waiting until later, petitioned for an election. They did not take seriously, however, the political techniques that El Paso's principal citizens had learned over the years. In accordance with the familiar pattern of elections held on the border, a battalion of Mexicans was imported to vote in favor of El Paso, receiving, of course, some kind of compensation for services rendered. Moreover, a number of El Pasoans voted several times; one of them, according to Owen White, cast twelve votes during the day while wearing a variety of disguises. Although the total number of registered voters in El Paso was known to be about three hundred, as many as two thousand votes were cast by midafternoon. Ysleta's protest proved futile, and the political influence that Mexican-Americans had formerly exercised now shifted to the Anglo business and professional establishment of El Paso. A significant statistic dramatizes this transfer of local political power—while five Mexican-Americans held the office of county judge before 1883, not one has held the position for almost a hundred years.[64]

When the railroad to El Paso bypassed San Elizario, it left area farmers at a serious disadvantage, though this circumstance was not universally lamented. As a result they shifted from the cultivation of fruits during the 1880s to grains, particularly wheat and corn, which were less perishable and easier to transport. By 1888 the American side of the El Paso valley had evolved from a fruit- and vegetable-producing region to one where grains now reigned supreme. At the same time, on the Mexican side the Mission grape remained. There an acre with one thousand vines was worth a thousand dollars, and during the three-month harvest season, at least three carloads of grapes crossed each day from Mexico to the American side for shipment to various points in the United States.[65]

By 1888 El Paso had eight thousand inhabitants, and El Paso del Norte (renamed Ciudad Juárez that year) had twelve thousand. This burgeoning population led to a growing concern on both sides of the border about an adequate water supply for the future. Not only was a greater amount of water being taken from the river in Colorado and New Mexico, but local demand was also rising. In 1888 Anson Mills proposed the construction of a dam three miles above El Paso. The structure, about 60 feet high and 450 feet wide, would create a lake in the Upper Valley that would provide irrigation water for about 200,000 acres of valley land. The plan provoked a howl of protest from the residents of the Mesilla Valley, Las Cruces, and Doña Ana. By this time the Mexican government had entered the picture with complaints that diversion of water from the river, which was international in character, was causing great damage to crops and farms on the Mexican side. Significantly the Mills project came to be known as the International Dam, but bill after bill in Congress supporting the project passed the Senate only to be voted down in the House of Representatives.[66]

Meanwhile, in November 1888 Colonel George B. Stevenson submitted his own plan, which was unfavorably received in the Lower Valley. Supporters in El Paso accepted it enthusiastically, however, and organized the El Paso Irrigation Company, which contracted with the Rosenfield Construction Company of Denver to build a canal. The contract called for the erection of a dam across the river about two hundred yards below the old Mexican dam, with suitable headgates for the canal just above it. The canal was to follow the left bank of the river, then along Eighth Street for nineteen blocks, then turn northward for eleven or twelve blocks to pass around the bend in the river forming Cordova Island. After going back to the east for three miles, it would then move on in a straight course parallel to the river for twenty-three miles and terminate near Fabens. After many delays, the canal was finally completed in 1891.[67]

Beginning in the late 1880s most of the town council meetings in San Elizario were devoted to the water and irrigation problem. After completion of the Franklin Canal, with the substantial sums the owners charged for water rights, the council enacted a municipal tax ordinance on 8 May 1891. It included a forty-six-item form to

be filled out by any "person, firm, company, or corporation within the corporate limits of San Elizario." Residents labeled it an outrage and forced the council to terminate the incorporation. For the time being the local acequia became the sole source of water.[68]

By mid-1893 the people of San Elizario decided to give incorporation another try. The town had a population of more than a thousand and could be incorporated as a city, which would give the council additional powers over taxation and make it more difficult for the voters to abolish the corporation. The city of San Elizario then renewed relations with the owners of the Franklin Canal. Yet, as Alice White has noted, throughout the troubled history of the canal the operators "failed to win over a large percent of the valley people to full confidence in its promises, and they failed to unite the will and energy of these people in a firm determination to make the enterprise a success." The Franklin Canal, as viewed by the valley people, "was an alien-controlled innovation that treated water rights and water assessments in terms of dollars rather than" service.[69]

In the mid-1890s the problem of sufficient irrigation water in the valley became critical. Water began to fail in the ditches, there were crop failures in 1895 and 1896, and the desperate San Elizario farmers were forced to plant alfalfa whose roots penetrated to a depth of thirteen feet. As conditions continued to deteriorate, the *El Paso Times* daily emphasized the pressing need for a local dam, pointing out that the agricultural interests of the entire area would be destroyed over time if the depleted river flow were not corrected.[70]

During the spring of 1897, travelers and train crews arriving from the north repeatedly warned of the gathering waters in the upper Rio Grande basin. In late April there were widespread reports that snowbanks in the mountains of New Mexico and Colorado were the heaviest on record and that the rivers of New Mexico were abnormally swollen. The *El Paso Times* warned that a flood was coming and that El Paso should be prepared for it, but no action was taken. The expected floodwaters arrived in El Paso on the night of 8 May, broke through the banks of the Franklin Canal, and by morning the smelter just north of the city was under four feet of water. The flood paralyzed El Paso, Ciudad Juárez, and the Lower Valley for an entire month. It washed away all the canal banks, levees, and headgates. Scores of homes were inundated, thousands of people evacuated, and crops on the most productive farms destroyed. San Elizario's losses from being bypassed by the railroad in 1881 were nothing compared to those resulting from the flood of 1897. Farmers by the scores left to try to find employment elsewhere. If there was anything that dramatized the pressing need for a dam, this was it, but Elephant Butte Dam was not completed until 1916, nineteen years later.[71]

G. A. Martin graphically depicted the ruins and remains of historic San Elizario in a 1923 article written for the *El Paso Herald* entitled "Old San Elizario—Home of the Salt War and the Finest Wine in the World." Although only a few old buildings at San Elizario were well preserved, he wrote, a true connecting link between the past and the present was the old church, completed in 1887, which was in good repair and attractive and appealing from the outside. There were the remains of the building known as Los Portales, which had been initially erected as a private home, then used as the first county courthouse, and later as a school. Then there were ruins of the Loretto Academy, the first school in West Texas, which had remained in San Elizario since its founding in 1879 until it was moved to El Paso in 1892. Other ruins were J. M. Luján's home, Gaspar Girón's grist mill, and the buildings on what was at one time the main street of the town. Yet, the completion of Elephant Butte Dam, Martin noted, had brought something of a revival. "There is water again," he said, "and farming all about the old town. Fields that once were the home of the famous grape are cleared again, and the workmen often find evidence of the old acequias that irrigated the vineyards and are now planted to cotton and alfalfa." He concluded, "Of all the places close to El Paso, old San Elizario, once the county seat of El Paso County, probably holds more memories of stirring events for pioneers than any other. Hanging over the old town is more glamour and more history and more of interest than about any other locality in the country."[72]

Fifty years later the theme of faded glory appealed to another observer. Writing in 1973, Eugene O. Porter concluded his paean to the glorious history of San Elizario as follows:

> San Elizario, isolated, slipped back into the stream of historical anonymity—a picturesque little village with ruins of a civilization that is gone forever. *Sic transit gloria.*[73]

The writer's judgment—highly poetic though it was—was largely inaccurate. Today, San Elizario and the ancient communities of Ysleta and Socorro are heroically struggling to preserve their histories, as embodied in the missions of Corpus Christi de Ysleta and Purísima Concepción de Socorro and the church in San Elizario, standing on the original site of the military chapel of the long-vanished presidio. Without doubt, we have a deeper understanding of that history than at any time in the recent past. Sadly, the "picturesque little village" is also gone. In its place is a rapidly growing community that faces a serious challenge if it is successfully to impart to new arrivals a sense of the history of the place. When those new to the area chance to use the local telephone book or study the stained-glass windows in the church on the plaza, they will have an encounter with the history of San Elizario. With the presidio came soldiers named Escageda, Olguín, Montes, Ronquillo, and Sambrano. They and their families, among others, laid the foundation of modern San Elizario.

¡Viva San Elizario!

DOCUMENTARY APPENDIX

Inspection of the Presidio of San Elizario*

Presidial troops of
Nueva Vizcaya Cavalry
Royal Presidio of San Elizario, May 1790

Extract of the review and inspection that I, Lieutenant Colonel don Antonio Cordero, captain of the presidio of Janos and commissioned subinspector for the troops of the province of Nueva Vizcaya, conducted of the cavalry company that garrisons this presidio, from 10 to 13 May 1790.

Officers and Staff	Places
Capt. don Juan Antonio de Arce	1
Lt. don Marcos Reaño	1
1st Afz. don Antonio Arce	1
2nd Afz. don Mariano Varela	1
Chaplain Fray Juan Bermejo	1
Armorer José María Ramos	1
Drummer José Bustillos	1
Total	7

Troops	Places	Horses	Mules
Sgt. Diego Ronquillo	1	5	1
Sgt. Mariano Polanco	1	9	0
Corporals	3	18	1
Corporals	1	6	1
Riflemen	2	8	2
Riflemen	2	14	2
Privates	24	139	9
Privates	32	192	10
Total	66	391	26

This company has a complete complement of troops, which is 73, including officers, a chaplain, sergeants, armorer, and a drummer. Those proposed for retirement are one corporal, one rifleman, and one private, all of whom are creditors of the pension fund.

I have expedited permissions for six men who have completed their obligations and three who are unfit to serve. I am preparing to have them replaced with healthy recruits who have the characteristics required for service in these provinces.

The troop is in average shape, but gifted with the agility, vigor, and calm to acquire all necessary training and discipline, which it lacks at present. In the military exercises and maneuvers I witnessed, the only skill I noted was in target practice.

The company captain, don Juan Antonio de Arce, though he has aptitude, does not apply it to encourage training as this job requires. For this reason, and because of his lack of vigor and his illnesses, he does not keep good order. I have admonished him about these particulars, and the warnings seem to have been productive.

The lieutenant, don Marcos de Reaño, is a strong officer, ready for service on campaign and for garrison duty, though he has an agitated nature.

The 1st alferez, don Antonio de Arce, manifests spirit and the readiness that is most required to be useful because he has received training and is healthy. At present he is involved with the interests of the company since he is the paymaster. He keeps good records. At the same time, he has the commission for the construction of the new presidio, recently moved to Los Tiburcios.

The 2nd alferez, don Mariano Varela, is an officer who applies himself and is precise and punctual.

The father chaplain, fray Juan Bermejo, served for the last twelve years in the presidios of Santa Fe, New Mexico, and in [San Elceario]. His is indiscreet, and there is little about him to make it worthwhile keeping him here.

The troops of this company are dedicated to the defense of the pueblos of El Paso del Río del Norte, which are contiguous to the present site of the presidio. They are equally occupied on campaign, contributing detachments provided for that reason; protecting the horse herd in their care; and guarding the goods of the fields belonging to the citizenry of El Paso.

The service-record book is up-to-date.

The armament is in good order, complete but for the lack of twelve leather jackets and two braces of pistols, which I have ordered replaced.

With respect to the large articles of clothing, the uniforms are complete and in average condition, but many small items indispensable for campaign duty are missing. I have informed the captain that he should not fail to see that everyone in the company has bags for pinole, napkins, flasks, bottles, and other utensils. He is also to take care that the troops are provided with them by means of a weekly inspection, during which he should see that they have them. I am also arranging for him to provide for the care of the troops' families, who have been neglected.

The riding gear of the troops is complete but barely serviceable.

The horse herd consists of 391 horses: 11 individuals have 7 horses each, 34 have 6 each, and the others have 4 or 5. There are 26 men who have 1 mule each. As a result the company lacks 85 horses and 41 mules to fulfill its complement of 7 horses and 1 mule for each man. The existing herd is in good shape for service.

In the accounting made for this company at the end of April of the present year, the troops earned 5,317 pesos 1 real 3⅜ granos, from which 615 pesos 3 reales 6½ granos have been deducted for what seven individuals owe. I have approved the accounting because there is no protest from the troops and have determined that the administrative charges have been arrived at fairly.

I have also approved the Gratification Fund accounts that run from the end of 1789, because they are accurate and legal. They exist in the form of a promissory note to the paymaster and not in cash because they are invested in other concerns of the company: 365 pesos 7 reales 2¼ granos.

The accounts and distribution of gunpowder running until the end of this year are accurate, and I approved them. There remained 2 quintals 6 [libras] of priming powder and 2 quintals 2 arrobas 2½ [libras] of ordinary gunpowder. They brought 2 arrobas of priming powder and 3½ of the ordinary gunpowder as an allotment at the beginning of the year. The current distribution is made from the total amount.

The drummer is neither skillful nor does he play properly. In order to provide him, as well as the other drummers in the province who are equally backward, with training, I therefore propose an assembly that will bring them all into line. He has a drum equipped with everything necessary for its use.

The tobacco monopoly and the mail are the paymaster's responsibility. He manages them in accord with the regulations he has received from the respective directors.

San Elizario, 13 May 1790
Antonio Cordero [rúbrica]

*AGS, Guerra Moderna 7047:52.

Service Record of Marcos Reaño*

Lieutenant Marcos Reaño, age forty-eight, native of Reinosa (Cantabria, Spain), of noble status, robust, service and circumstances as follows:

Dates of service in each position				Time of service in each position			
Position	Days	Months	Years	Position	Years	Months	Days
Private	28	Jan.	1757	Private	14	7	2
Corporal	1	May	1772	Corporal	4	9	10
Sergeant	1	Feb.	1777	Sergeant	1	4	25
2nd alferez	26	Oct.	1778	2nd alferez	1	3	17
1st alferez	14	Oct.	1779	1st alferez	8	6	14
Lieutenant	29	Apr.	1788	Lieutenant	2	8	2

Total to the end of December 1790: 33 years, 3 months

Regiments in which he has served

In the Belgian Dragoons in Spain, whence he came to this kingdom in don Juan Villalba's expedition in order to join the Spanish Dragoons, he has served as a private, grenadier, and corporal. He rose to the rank of sergeant of the presidio of San Carlos, and from there went on to become 2nd and 1st alferez of the presidios of Carrizal and San Buenaventura. He is currently lieutenant of the presidio of San Elizario.

Campaigns and battles he has participated in

He took part in the entire Portuguese campaign and in the expedition to Sonora, personally participating in every campaign undertaken there, in particular that of Cerro Prieto. There he led his men to rescue his colonel, don Domingo Elizondo, and removed him from several difficult situations. He has been attacked twice while in command of the royal horse herd and defended it with his troops against a large enemy force. He has participated in eight campaigns under the command of various leaders

and other officers during which, as has been verified, he killed thirty-seven and captured fifty-two of the enemy. He accompanied the adjutant inspector, don Diego de Borica, on his inspection tours in the capacity of assistant inspector of the troops. He went on a foray with forty men and captured five of the enemy. He had an encounter with a large enemy force and while defending himself with only ten men, prevented the enemy from carrying off a single animal. With one cadet and four citizens, he recovered from the enemy some oxen they had stolen. He went on a campaign that managed to kill fifteen and capture thirty of the enemy, recovering a like number of animals. He went on a foray that recovered fifty animals and other spoils. On another sortie he recovered a stolen horse. He took part in three campaigns that captured eight of the enemy, recovering forty animals from them. He was commissioned to work on the peace with the Gila Apaches. He participated in three campaigns, two under the command of the commandant of the division, don Antonio Cordero, and the other under the command of Captain don Ramón Marrujo. With a detachment of eighty men, he reconnoitered the Sierra del Gallego; when the enemy attacked, four soldiers went in pursuit. In the current year, 1790, he led a campaign under his own command that attacked the enemy and recovered from them what they had stolen.

Juan Antonio de Arce [rúbrica]

Inspector's Report	Notes
He is a good officer.	His valor is known.
	He applies himself.
	He has average ability.
	His conduct is good.
	He is married.
	Arce [rúbrica].

*AGS, Guerra Moderna 7278:8.

Instructions to be observed by the commandants of outposts charged with dealing with the Apache Indians who are currently at peace in various places in Nueva Vizcaya and with those who may seek it in the future:*

1. The officers charged with dealing with the Apaches who are at peace and those who may come to seek it will find a much recommended merit in the execution of their commission, which essentially consists of being very prudent in order to avoid mistakes in the pursuit of so important a matter.

2. On no account will they fail to demonstrate good faith with the Apaches or regarding anything promised them. The officer in charge is to impress this way of thinking on his subalterns so that they do not stray from it. So that no one deviates from this, anyone who attempts deception will be punished. In this way the Apaches will see that such behavior is not tolerated among the Spaniards.

3. The Indians' crude and gross ways are to be tolerated and their impertinences overlooked despite the inconveniences they may cause. The Spaniards are to get to know the Apaches not only to draw them in but also to learn their secret intentions. Because it is of great interest for the Indians to remain in Spanish camps on the frontier

and for others to join them, the officer in charge is given the special responsibility of carefully managing the Apaches' arrogant and delicate character. This is so that they do not suddenly run away and commit more excesses. To prevent their rebellion, it is considered advantageous not to dissuade them from the zeal that reigns among the different rancherias or factions established at each post. This is to be done in such a way that they never break with or attack one another so long as they are living under Spanish protection.

4. The officer in charge is to designate one of the capitancillos of the rancherias at peace as judge in the first instance and leader of his people. This is so that the capitancillos will be able to impose the punishment they deem appropriate, should crimes against the tranquility of the post occur or on those occasions when it may be necessary to make a public example. That way, the Indians will be more likely to accept it. If there is a loyal capitancillo of outstanding character in a group of several rancherias, he is to be named overall leader, with [Nava's] knowledge. This has been done with El Compá at Janos presidio. The Spaniards will accord these capitancillos more respect than normal and give them gifts, which they esteem greatly, but are of little value.

5. Indians at peace are neither to attack Spanish troops or citizenry nor damage their goods. In matters of little consequence, the capitancillo of the rancheria of the perpetrator will be notified so that he can punish him as he sees fit and return what has been stolen. In serious cases the officer in charge is to proceed cautiously, keeping the appropriate judgment in mind and without calling attention to anyone. If the circumstances call for it, he may at times overlook the crime, either because of a shortage of forces at the post or because the officer realizes that no greater damage can come from those Indians.

6. If any Indians at the posts openly revolt, those who remain loyal should be encouraged to join Spanish troops in pursuing them. The Spaniards will remain calm in order to convince those Indians who stay behind that they look with disdain on Indians who are disloyal and that they will be punished and reduced again.

7. The Spaniards will have frequent conferences with the capitancillos in the presence of their warriors and women. This is to inspire humane thinking and a civil society among them. They are to be shown how many advantages they will gain by giving up their errant ways, which are full of needs and iniquities, and embracing a calm, sure peace under Spanish protection.

8. The officers in charge will apply themselves and learn the Apache language. They will also instruct their subalterns, sergeants, and others with an aptitude for languages. Children of the troops are to be encouraged to

play with Apache youngsters so that they too can learn Apache. This practice will lead to mutual confidence that will be difficult to uproot. In this way, the officers will not need to rely on interpreters who do not always tell the Indians what they are told, either because they do not understand, being generally simple men, or for their own reasons. Even an officer's poorly given speech will have greater impact than an interpreter's clearest translation.

9. The officer in charge will explain in detail to the capitancillos that among the Spaniards there are good and bad men, some of whom may influence them to do things against peace and harmony. Whenever the Indians encounter such mischief and suspicious behavior, they will have the officer in charge and other officers clarify the situation, which they will do in short order. This must be insisted upon because of the recent example of Pascual Ruiz and the Indians at peace in Carrizal and other places.

10. The officer in charge will have Apaches at peace pursue those at war against the Spaniards first alone and then in the company of Spanish troops. They will force the enemy to sue for peace or bring them back as prisoners. Before undertaking such expeditions, the enemy rancherias are to be reconnoitered to determine what territory they occupy, who their capitancillos are, how many warriors they have, and whether there are any other rancherias nearby. To this end, a few loyal Indians, either alone or with soldiers, will be sent to that place, which will be carefully selected. With such precautions, the expeditions are assured of success.

11. Whether the Indians at peace execute the reconnaissance alone or with Spanish troops, under no circumstances are they to capture the enemy under the pretext of peace. War will be waged on the enemy vigorously, but without such tricks.

12. When the officer in charge has reliable news that the enemy is within 20, 30, or 40 leagues of his post, he will to mete out punishment without delay, taking advantage of all available auxiliaries so that the strike will not fail. When circumstances permit, however, he will inform the division commandant beforehand. He, in turn, will inform [Nava], unless the delay is prejudicial.

13. Apache men will be allowed to hunt on their own horses, leaving their families on the land they designate for their rancherias. This is so that the Spaniards can watch them and their movements and do nothing to harm them.

14. Indian men will be allowed to visit their relatives and friends at other posts, but must leave their families behind. They will be permitted to go make mescal and gather the fruits that sustain them.

15. As a general rule, Indians at peace traveling 10 leagues from their post will be given documents or a pass-

port, whether they are going hunting, visiting friends, or reconnoitering land where the enemy may be. In this way, Spanish detachments will not harm them, and they will become accustomed to being subordinated, which is something they did not understand among themselves before the Spaniards arrived. The officer in charge or his substitute will always sign the passports. They will state which Apaches are going, for what reason, by what route, and for how long they have permission. It is considered useful to record all their names as well.

16. The abusive practice of returning prisoners that Spanish troops or Indian auxiliaries capture to the Indians at peace will be halted. The Indians at peace will not claim prisoners taken on the field of battle because they are the true enemy. For this reason they must be removed from land where they can be dangerous, even to the Indians at peace. Experience has proved this to be all too true with a number of captives who were freed, only to commit new acts of hostility. If a capitancillo who has repeatedly proved his loyalty earnestly requests the return of a woman or child, [Nava] is to be informed so that he can decide, but officers will not make promises they have no authority to fulfill. Prisoners will be treated humanely and gently. They will be provided with what they need to eat, but kept secure so that they cannot escape. They will be delivered as quickly as possible to Chihuahua.

17. Apaches at peace will not be allowed to travel to Chihuahua to ask for freedom for prisoners or for any other reason. The only exception will be an urgent and obvious case bearing on general peace and harmony or that of a particular post. In such a situation, the officers in charge will allow one of the most highly respected capitancillos to go, accompanied by the smallest possible number of his people. Whenever possible, [Nava] will be asked if the trip is necessary and his response awaited.

18. When capitancillos request peace, it will be granted with the following conditions. First, the Indians will give up their errant, wicked ways and live in peace under Spanish protection. Second, they will be assigned land near the post, so that their rancherias can be frequently inspected. They will be made to understand the advantage that will result from being located near the post, principally that they will not risk being attacked by troops from other posts who do not know they are at peace. Third, the Indians will be told clearly about the assistance the Spaniards will provide for their sustenance until such time as they can feed themselves. Fourth, they will go promptly on any expedition the Spaniards contemplate against the enemy. In that case, and in no other, they will be supplied with as many horses as necessary from those designated for that purpose. Finally, as for the written permission to go hunting and visiting, it will be enforced so that no one

can justly protest bad faith on the Spaniards' part.

19. In order to avoid surprises, each officer in charge will befriend one or more individuals from each rancheria by means of small gifts. Through these confidants it will be possible to learn the Indians' innermost thoughts. Interpreters and others who know Apache are to frequent the rancherias, artfully trying to find out whether there is any plot against Spanish interests so they can report it immediately. These warnings, however, will only serve to further the investigation of their veracity, since hasty action could result in irreparable harm. The Indians at peace should never see mistrust, which might alienate them from their friendship with the Spaniards.

20. The foregoing article notwithstanding, caution is required when dealing with the Apaches. Those who have blindly trusted them have repented their decision at great cost because of the Indians' fickleness and other pernicious qualities. Even though the Apaches have given the Spaniards repeated proof of their friendship, those in command are advised to remain distrustful, ever vigilant that the discipline of the troops and watchfulness of the post and horse guards never waver. They will keep their weapons loaded at all times, and each soldier will have the appropriate number of cartridges. This measure will contain any plot against the Spaniards.

21. Every week each Apache male who has a wife will be given 2 almudes of maize or wheat, 4 boxes of cigarettes, 1 piloncillo, 1/2 prinado of salt, and 1 ration of meat (when available). The meat ration is to be 1/32, which is how beefs are divided. If the Indian is a capitancillo, his portion will be increased by an another piloncillo and two additional boxes of cigarettes. Each additional adult in a family will be given one-half of a family portion; a boy or girl under the age of thirteen will receive one-quarter, and nursing children nothing. Children under seven will not be given cigarettes.

22. Capitancillos, their favorite wives, or anyone with status among them will be given clothing and riding gear. Those who distinguish themselves in battle will also be rewarded. Nevertheless, commandants should proceed in this matter with the greatest possible economy, such that what they give the Indians is of little value but highly esteemed.

23. Weekly supplies will be given in every post on Mondays. Only Apaches living within the wall of the post or within 2 to 4 leagues at most are eligible. Those who have rancherias farther away will be given what is prudently thought to be convenient, with an eye to their needs and how they have acted. This will be left up to the judgment of the officers in charge. In order to attract Apaches closer to the posts, they will be given some little something and allowed to see how many more supplies are given to Indians who join the Spaniards with complete confidence.

24. An account book of distributions to the Apaches at peace will be kept. The date of weekly rations and the families who receive them will be recorded. In order to provide something to individuals from the rancherias that are more than 4 leagues away, to Indians who seek peace, or to give some gift of clothing, a draft or voucher from the commandant to the paymaster is needed. The paymaster will keep the account book, a copy of which he will submit for inspection every six months. The officer in charge and the paymaster should sign it. In this way, the accounting will make its way to [Nava].

25. When Indians at peace go on campaign, they will be given the most lightweight provisions they can easily carry. In addition to cigarettes, they will take sufficient provisions so that they will not halt operations and withdraw before punishing the enemy. Every possible economy should be sought in the distribution of provisions.

26. As a general rule, each officer in charge will report the exact number of people in each rancheria, noting how many are married; the number of young men, women, and children; and the number of animals. This report will be submitted to the general command each month. The territory that each rancheria occupies should be specified, as well as the distance from the principal post. Those making mescal or hunting and the direction they take are to be noted. All this should be done with the Apaches' knowledge, given their natural mistrust.

27. The Apaches resort to stealing livestock from Spanish camps because of their needs. They require animals for hunting and sustenance. In view of this, to avoid destruction of the meager goods in the countryside, and to make them happy, it is considered absolutely necessary for their rancherias to be brought near Spanish frontier posts. So that they will become civilized, they will embrace the Catholic religion and work for their sustenance as other civilized people do. Permitting them to live in distant rancherias runs the risk that they will continue their thefts and errant lifestyle without becoming civilized, since the Spaniards cannot observe their movements. Thus every effort should be made to force them to draw near the Spaniards. First, kindness and persuasion should be employed so they will settle on the fertile land the Spaniards will supply until such time as they can live from their work, to which women and children will progressively apply themselves. As for the warriors, it is doubtful that they will do that kind of work even after a long time. This is because they live in idleness and are only suited for war.

28. Based on the arguments expressed in the previous article, [Nava] warns the officers in charge to obtain from the Apaches at peace exact information about the rancherias they know of, such as where they are usually located, the names of their capitancillos, the number of warriors they have, what they subsist on, and where they

most frequently make war. Having taken these precautions, the officers in charge will send quick-witted emissaries of good faith from among the Indians at peace to the rancherias to invite them to draw near the Spaniards. This is so that they can take advantage of the tranquility that the Spaniards' protection affords. Even when they cannot persuade them, the Indians at peace will acquire information needed to take appropriate measures. They should be well informed of the Spaniards' honest and upright intentions. This is so that they can inform the enemy capitancillos, warriors, and women, demonstrating the calm and tranquility they and their families enjoy, as well as the support given to those who live quietly near the Spaniards.

29. Whenever one or more rancherias request peace, it will be granted on an interim basis under the conditions expressed in article 18. In the presence of all the officers, the site closest to the post that can provide adequate land and water will be designated. With proper care, the assistance they are to be given will be reduced over time. [Nava] is to be informed about everything related to this matter so that he can make appropriate decisions.

30. If after trying gentle methods the emmissaries fail to achieve their aim of attracting nearer to the post distant rancherias that are not at peace, they will be considered and treated as the enemy with respect to the hostilities that, by necessity, they commit in Spanish territory to obtain their sustenance.

31. Trade in anything but unbranded livestock with Indians who seek peace or those who have already accepted it is forbidden. This will remove from Indians who have yet to seek peace the incentive to steal livestock.

32. The gradual reduction of increased expenses to the royal treasury for the Indians' sustenance is the responsibility of the officer in charge. For that reason he is to settle Apaches at peace and those who seek peace on the land best suited for planting and dry farming maize and on irrigable land when it is available. They will see the lands are their own and develop a love of them. They should be encouraged to build jacales and plant pumpkins and melons. In this way they will come to appreciate the fruit of their meager labor. Some land is suited for raising cattle. If any Indians show an inclination for this activity, the officers in charge are to inform [Nava] and relate to him their opinions and the permanency they think that that industry might have.

33. There is no reason to think that men accustomed only to war and hunting will dedicate themselves to such work, but the women and children may. This is especially the case when they are shown the example of Spaniards working a plot of land where 1 or 2 almudes of maize are sown. The plot is to be cultivated until the ears appear. Before they ripen, the field should be given to the leader of the rancheria so that he and his people can care for it.

At harvest time, they should gather the maize, store it, and use it among themselves. The following year, they can be given a larger field when the time for preparing it comes. In this way, they will move progressively toward doing all the work themselves.

34. Since Apache women are hard workers, the officer in charge can give them and their children some wage labor, either in the fields at planting, irrigation, preparation, or harvest time or grinding pinole or flour for the troops. Those with a financial interest in the matter should punctually pay the Indians a fair wage in the presence of an officer, so that they will not be exploited. The good conduct of the officer in charge and the soldiers' positive example, together with some timely given piloncillo and cigarettes, will triumph over difficulties that seemed insurmountable to those unwilling to dedicate themselves to contributing effectively to the solid establishment of these Indians, upon which the tranquility of those provinces depends.

35. Every officer in charge should entreat and charge the post chaplain not to interfere in the governing of the Apache Indians. He should carry out his ministry with the judiciousness and prudence their unformed nature requires. The time will come when they are more civilized and will take advantage of his gentle admonitions to embrace the Catholic religion. In the meantime, gentleness is needed to avoid exasperating them, lest they return to their errant, wicked ways.

36. Officers in charge will make known anything they think will help produce the ends expressed in these instructions. If they find something in them that is not appropriate for their territory or contrary to the aim of encouraging the Apaches to establish and consolidate peace, they are required to make it known. If any officer in charge lacks the necessary knowledge, constancy, temperament, or other characteristics called for to fulfill so delicate a responsibility, he should inform [Nava]. This is to be done to avoid any difficulty that may result from the situation over time.

37. Finally, because the matter is so much in the interest of the royal service, the officers in charge must take great pains to carry out these instructions vigorously and prudently. This will be of great use to them as far as future promotions are concerned. They are to give copies of these instructions to all officers for their information, and they are to be read frequently to sergeants and corporals.

Chihuahua, 14 October 1791
Pedro de Nava

*Pedro de Nava, Instructions for dealing with the Apaches at peace in Nueva Vizcaya, Chihuahua, 14 Oct. 1791, JA II, r. 13, 1788, bk. 1, f. 325–49. Another copy is in AGI, Guadalajara 289.

Mateo Montes Land Grant*

Don Andrés Mateos, lieutenant and commandant of cavalry of this royal presidio of San Elizario

Mateo Montes appeared before me to request a plot of land to build a house where he could live. After considering the matter, I decided that it was a good idea to give him a plot next to the wall. North to south it measures sixty varas; east to west it measures sixty varas. It is bounded on the east by land belonging to Mariano Alvarado, on the west by royal lands, on the north by the road that follows along the front of the wall, and on the south by the acequia. In the name of his majesty (may God keep him) and by virtue of my authority, I grant it to him in perpetuity for himself, his children, and descendants, so that he can build his house and live there in peaceful quietude by virtue of this grant. For this reason I gave him this document, copied from the registry in my charge where these titles are recorded. So that this may be of record, I signed with two attending witnesses on 22 April 1803.

Andrés Mateos [rúbrica]

Attending   Attending
Vicente Valdés [rúbrica]   Luciano Márquez [rúbrica]

*Personal papers of Samuel Sánchez, Sr.

Urban Cavalry Company of San Elizario   **Department of Chihuahua***

List of individuals in the above company with a count of the weapons, mounts, ammunition, and remounts they have as of today's date.

Classes	Names	Rifles	Lances	Arrows	Cartridges	Flints	Mounts	Remounts
Captain	José Ignacio Ronquillo	1			45	3	1	2
Lieutenant	Juan Pedro Pérez	1			45	3	1	2
Alferez	José Cartagena	1			15	1	1	1
Sergeant	Santos Lucero	1	1		5	1	1	1
Corporal	Crescencio Montes	1			4	1	1	1
	Juan Bustillos	1			6	1	1	1
	Francisco Varela	1			6	1	1	1
	Nepomuceno Loya	1			5	1	1	1
Private	Bernabé Pérez	1	1		5	1	1	
	José Pérez I		1				1	1
	Hipólito Ortiz		1				1	
	José Alarcón	1			1	1	1	1
	Compasión Gándara	1			15	1	1	1
	Marcelino Chaves	1	1		10	1	1	1
	Julián Rueda			10			1	
	Juan Carrasco	1			3	1	1	
	José Montes	1			4	1	1	1
	Manuel Frésquez			15			1	1
	Cirilo Olguín	1			3	1	1	1
	Gregorio Estrada	1			10	1	1	1
	Cipriano Maese	1			6	1	1	1

Classes	Names	Rifles	Lances	Arrows	Cartridges	Flints	Mounts	Remounts
	Romualdo Gutiérrez	1	1		6	1	1	1
	Ramón Gándara	1	1		5	1	1	1
	Andrés Olguín	1				1	1	1
	Mariano Maese	1				1	1	1
	Jacinto Gómez	1			9	1	1	1
	José Jurado	1	1		3	1	1	1
	Patricio Maese	1	1				1	
	Luis Gándara	1	1			1	1	1
	Gregorio Gándara	1			5	1	1	1
	José Loya	1				1	1	1
	José Chávez		1				1	1
	Martín García	1			15	1	1	1
	Caetano Onopa		1	15			1	1
	Joaquín Gándara	1			5	1	1	1
	Ignacio Escorza	1				1	1	1
	Felipe López	1			2	1	1	1
	José Luján	1				1	1	1
	Carlos Guerra	1			15	2		
	Amadeus Navarrete		1					
	Trinidad García	1	1		15	1	1	2
	Epitanio Sánchez	1				3	1	1
	Antonio Loya	1			2	1	1	1
	Juan Sánchez	1					1	
	Esteban Fajes	1			15	1	1	1
	Juan Sierra		1				1	
	José Sambrano		1				1	

Classes	Names	Rifles	Lances	Arrows	Cartridges	Flints	Mounts	Remounts
	Jesús Luján	1			15	1	1	1
	Tomás Carrasco	1	1			1	1	1
	Rafael Gómez		1				1	
	José Pérez II	1			10	1		
	José Berrú	1				1		
	Juan Mizeno	1			9	2	1	
	José Contreras	1				1	1	
	Juan Suárez			15			1	1
	José Antonio Arroyo	1	1		15	1	1	1
	Juan Arroyo	1	1		15	1	1	
	Santiago Berrú	1	1		3	1	1	1
	Juan José Luján							
	Cruciano Alvillán	1	1		15	1	1	1
	Cástulo Hidalgo	1	1		3	1	1	1
	Francisco Chávez	1				1	1	1
	Crescencio Roybal	1			6	1	1	1
	Sixto Guerra	1			15	1		
	Concepción Apodaca	1	1		7	1	1	1
	Total	52	24	55	398	57	59	51

San Elizario, November 1836
José Ignacio Ronquillo [rúbrica]

*JA I, r. 6, bk. 33, 1836, vol. 4.

Service Record of José Mízquiz*

Cavalry Company of San Elizario: José Mízquiz, son of Esteban [Mízquiz] and María Gertrudis Navarrete, and native of this presidio of San Elizario, farmer; five feet four inches seven lines tall; age twenty; and Roman Catholic. His physical characteristics include black hair and eyebrows, brown eyes, a normal nose, brown skin, no beard, and a scar on the left side of his head in the form of a "U."

On 1 November 1815 he enlisted voluntarily in this company for ten years. The regulations were read to him, and he was advised of the ordinances and additions to them. Because he did not know how to sign his name, he made the sign of a cross. He was advised that this justification would not serve as an excuse in any way. The witnesses were Corporal José Olguín and Private Francisco Arias, both from the same company.

He swore the loyalty oath and stated that he was not married.

Isidro Rey   José Olivares   Francisco Cáceres

———

By superior order of 22 December 1820 the most excellent lord captain general of these provinces, don Anastasio Bustamante, has declared that Article 12 of the regulations applies to this individual. There will be service awards on 21 March 1820 consisting of a medal given as an incentive for having joined for the Second Period the Army of the Three Guarantees of this empire, which pro-claimed the freedom of the fatherland on 27 August 1821. San Elizario, 3 February 1823.

———

The commandant general communicated the following declaration of the supreme government: By order of 24 February 1823, this individual is credited with five years, ten months, and twenty-seven days of double-time service on behalf of the independence of the nation from 1 November 1815 until 27 September 1821. San Elizario, 27 March 1824.

Olguín

———

This individual joined the Army of the Three Guarantees on 24 August 1821, at which time he recognized and proclaimed independence in the capital of this province, in accord with the order from the commandant general of 27 August 1821. He was not present in the ranks of the Army of the Three Guarantees when it entered into Mexico City because he was with his company. He also joined in the proclamation of freedom of 16 March 1823, which was circulated by means of an order for that end.

De Santa Cruz

———

Since 4 December 1824 he has received a bonus of 6 reales, which was declared by supreme order on 19 September 1829. The adjutant inspector applied this bonus to this company on 6 November 1829.

De Santa Cruz

———

In accord with the supreme order of the general congress of the union of 20 August 1829 and another issued by the president of the republic on 15 October 1829, this individual is credited with one month and eleven days of double-time service on campaign. San Elizario, 18 November 1829.

———

This individual has served as a corporal since 15 December 1829 on the recommendation of the captain of his company, don José María de Arce, and with the approval of the commandant general of 22 November 1829. San Elizario, 20 December 1829.

Arce

———

Since 22 November 1829 he has received a bonus of 9 reales, which was declared by supreme order of 22 April 1830. The adjutant inspector applied this bonus to this company on 9 June 1830. San Elizario, 16 June 1830.

Arce

———

On 29 September 1830 he participated in the battle in the Hueco Mountains under the command of Captain don José María Ronquillo. At that time they killed seventeen Comanche and Kiowa warriors, took one captive,

recovered eleven horses, and killed seven of the enemy's animals. San Elizario, 14 April 1831.

———

This individual participated in the battle at the Carrizo water hole under the command of Captain don José María Ronquillo on 29 November 1830. Seven Comanche warriors were killed, one was taken prisoner, and twenty-one horses were recovered. San Elizario, 14 April 1831.

———

This individual participated in the battle that Captain don José María Ronquillo led on 18 May 1836 in the Guadalupe Mountains against the Comanches. They killed two warriors, took four prisoners, and recovered sixteen horses and a few discarded items the Indians had left in their camp. San Elizario, 20 August 1836.

Parra

———

This individual participated in the battle under the command don José María de Arce at the outpost of Caseta on 18 May 183? during which they killed two Comanches and took from them what they had stolen. San Elizario, 1 January 1837.

Parra

———

This individual was under the command of Lieutenant don Antonio Parra in the battle with the Comanches at the water hole at the post on 18 April 1836. At that time they captured eight warriors and recovered three horses. San Elizario, 1 May 1837.

Parra

———

This individual participated in the battle that Sergeant (holding the rank of alferez), José Pérez led at the ford of ? in which they killed ten Comanche warriors and took from them everything they had stolen. San Elizario, 1 January 1837.

Parra

———

This individual reenlisted voluntarily for five more years at the time of the inspection held on 28 March 1837, when he received 20 pesos in cash and two months' furlough. The witnesses were the sergeants of this company, don Carlos Cáceres and Martín Sambrano. San Elizario, 28 March 1837.

Parra

———

This individual participated in the battle that Lieutenant Colonel don Caetano Justiniani led against the rebels of the Department of New Mexico on 27, 28, and 29 January 1838 during which they killed fifty-seven Indians and citizens. They left many of them for dead on the field of battle and won four plazas from the rebels. San Elizario, 2 April 1838.

Parra

By supreme order of 7 February 1838, which the adjutant inspector communicated to this company on 8 March 1838, this individual received a bonus of 9 reales and the rank of sergeant, beginning on 25 November 1834. San Elizario, 2 April 1838.

Parra

———

This individual participated in the fierce and bloody battle of the Sierra del Fierro. After it was contested from daybreak to nine or ten at night, the leader and officers managed an honorable withdrawal with thirty–two soldiers and twenty-one wounded. After a formal inquiry, the commandant general deemed the action heroic, and this individual received an immediate promotion to the rank he now holds. San Elizario, 15 January 1841.

Rey

———

The interested party participated under Alferez Félix Lerma's command in the battle of Ojo Caliente on 26 October 1841 during which one warrior and one Indian woman were killed. Thirty-two horses and eight mules were recovered, and we recorded other gains. San Elizario, 15 January 1841.

Rey

———

This individual was sentenced to a week of arrest for the crime of drunkenness, which he committed on 24 December 1840 upon leaving Carrizal. This was in accord with Article 26 of the penal law of 13 June 1838. He had to do this time because he had become unconscious and could not follow his company. This was treated as though it were a first offense, and he was warned that future offenses would bring about the punishment the law required for those who were absent from their duty. San Elizario, 16 January 1841.

Rey

———

This individual was promoted to sergeant of the company of Janos on 21 October 1841. From that day forward there was a vacancy in this company, since he had gone to his new post. The commandant general promoted him because of the merit he earned during the battle of the Sierra del Fierro. San Elizario, 1 November 1841.

Rey

———

Copy of the original that is in the book of service records of the company under my command, to which I attest. San Elizario, 23 June 1842.

Luis Rey [rúbrica]

*Janos Microfilm Collection, UTEP, roll 30.

San Elizario Lists for the Texas Campaign*

Detailed list of the citizens fit for war from the pueblo of San Elizario with a listing of their firearms and arrows, as well as of those who have none because they cannot afford them.

With Firearms

Name	Age
Jose Pérez	46
Crescencio Roybal	27
Tomás Orcasitas	46
Jesús Alarcón	18
Eluterio Lucero	40
Andrés Olguín	27
Anastacio Polanco	21
Ireneo Polanco	19
Nepomuceno Sambrano	28
Francisco Escageda	23
Jesús Medina	34
Hipólito Orcasitas	31
Trinidad García	49
Joaquín Molina	22
Elegio Sambrano	28
Rafael Almanza	30
Ignacio Aranda	49
José Loya	40

Name	Age
Patricio Loya	18
Esteban Palomares	40
Santiago Palomares	24
Victoriano Carrillo	25
Concepción Gándara	30
Epitanio Sánchez	33
José María Sánchez	20
Lino Guerra	17
Carlos Guerra	34
José Guerra	44
José Angel Jáquez	29
Felipe Valencia	26
Jesús Luján	35
Cipriano Ascárate	37
José María Rey	34
Antonio Loya	46
Juan López	28
Francisco Montes	31
José Ortega	43
Juan José Escageda	42
Severiano Olguín	26
Tomás Sánchez	30
Francisco Gómez	25
Nacario Gómez	22
Eusebio Gómez	20
Lorenzo Gómez	18

Name	Age	Name	Age
Guadalupe Gómez	32	Quirino Carrasco	32
Juan Luján	28	Manuel Herrera	42
Pedro Almangoa	30	José Ignacio Carrasco	60
Francisco Provencio	28	Francisco Vargas	51
Sabino Hidalgo	37	Juan Ruiz	49
Severiano Montes	28	José Jurado	52
Fermín Caballero	42	Gregorio Martínez	61
Martín García	40	Pedro Perú	57
Gonzalo Gándara	39	Santiago Berrú	59
José Moreno	30	Ramón Gándara	61
Patricio Maese	46	Ignacio Mestas	44
Luis Gándara	51	Clemente Varela	56
Pedro Gándara	26	José Apodaca	50
Juan Bustillos	47	Ramón Montes II	47
Gregorio García	31	José Ignacio Contreras	49
Erasmos Alvillán	54	José del Carmen Durán	55
Gregorio Alvillán	19	José Aguirre	36
Reyes Sambrano	32	Manuel Escageda	49
Ramón Lucero	46	Crescencio Montes	48
Toribio Lucero	27		89
Pánfilo Lucero	19		

With Bows and Arrows

Name	Age
Manuel Bustillos	29
Luis Madrid	40	Esteban Palomares	40
Anacleto Escageda I	28	Lino Guerra	18
Luis Sambrano	29	Narciso Loya	17
Jesús Sambrano	27	Vicente Lucero	30

Name	Age	Name	Age
Agapito Jercas	31	Eduviges Chávez	30
Cosme Maese	19	Simón Montes	29
Concepción Apodaca	29	Luis Ortiz	28
José María Berrú	28	Pedro Ortiz	26
Gregorio Apodaca	26	Martín Ortiz	20
Darío Perú	19	Antonio Ortiz	38
Quirino Armijo	30	Ricardo Ortiz	18
Bernardo Arias	31	Agapito Lara	24
Manuel Bello	50	Vicente Medina	23
	13	Gonzaga Medina	21
		Hipólito Luján	28

Men without weapons

Name	Age	Name	Age
Arcadio Loya	28	José María Polanco	22
Narciso Loya	19	Locadio Loya	27
José Olivares	41	Reduciendo Villalba	34
Carlos Bustillos	22	José María Berrú	29
Pablo Bustillos	20	Teodoro Sánchez	18
Saturnino Loya	31	Juan Apodaca	23
Esteban Lobato	19	Francisco Alvaza	40
Francisco Gándara	17	Gracia Ortiz	31
Ricardo Valencia	18	Hipólito Ortiz	34
Cleto Olguín	30	Pedro Ortiz	30
Juan José Sierra	42	Pedro Sisneros	30
Jesús Sierra	17	Romano Hidalgo	28
Luis Marrufo	31	Nicanor Pérez	20
		Felipe Suárez	23
		Jesús Escageda	27

Name	Age	Name	Age
Anacleto Escageda II	24	Sostenor Beltrán	31
Teodoro Perea	40	Quirino Archuleta	43
Doroteo Domínguez	41	Dionisio Trujillo	40
José Cadena	29	Andrés Luján	49
Hermenegildo Cadena	20	Cruz Rodríguez	38
Perfecto Ortiz	18	Félix Rodríguez	39
Cirilo Onopa	17	Sergio Valencia	51
Anastasio Domínguez	25	Ramón Olivas	70
Pedro Sánchez	45	León Perú	57
Jesús Almangoa	57	Basilio Rincón	42
Eustacio Castro	42	Ramón Luján	43
Dolores Madrid	41	Doroteo Luján	55
José María Archuleta	32	Juan Suárez	48
Juan Padilla	47	Julián Apodaca	60
Leandro Haro	38	Cipriano Lucero	52
Cornelio Frésquez	30	José María Onopa	56
Doroteo Luján	50	Cornelio Alvillán	41
Bautista Gándara	41	Juan Provencio	60
Geraldo Carvajal	30	Blas Chávez	51
José Polanco	49	Jesús Durán	18
Onofre Olguín	18	Luciano Varela	17
Juan de Haro	27	José María Frésquez	21
José Grijalba	39	Tomás Quintana	27
José Núñez	32		88
Miguel Trujillo	27		
José Chávez	32		

Summary

With firearms	89
With bows and arrows	13
Total	190

San Elizario, 31 May 1846

Gregorio Gándara [rúbrica]

JA II, r. 35, bk. 1, 1846, f. 252–57.

ENDNOTES

PREFACE

1. Rick Hendricks, "Presidio," in *Encyclopedia of Latin American History and Culture*, ed. Barbara A. Tenenbaum, (New York, 1996), 4:468–69.

2. Throughout this book we employ the modern spelling, San Elizario, which is generally thought to be a corruption by English speakers of the Spanish Elceario. In historical documents the name was spelled a variety of ways, most commonly Elezeario. The name was first given, undoubtedly by a Franciscan, to the Valley of San Elceario. The presidio that had been at Gajoquilla, near present-day Jiménez, Chihuahua, was moved to the valley of San Elceario in 1774, and in 1789 some thirty-seven miles upriver to the site of present-day San Elizario, Texas.

   St. Elzear of Sabran, Baron of Ansouis, Count of Ariano, was born in Ansouis in Provence in 1285. He studied under his uncle, William of Sabran, Abbot of St. Victor's in Marseilles. He wed Delphine of Glandèves, but the couple lived a virginal union. Elzear joined the Third Order of St. Francis. Upon his father's death in 1309, Elzear led an army to Italy to take up the lordship of Ariano, subduing his subjects through his kindness. He went on to Rome and assisted in the expulsion of the Emperor Henry VII. In 1317 he became the tutor of Charles, Duke of Naples, and subsequently his prime minister. Elzear was sent as ambassador to France in 1323; he died in Paris on 27 September of that year and was buried in Franciscan habit at the Minor Conventual Church at Apt. His godson, Urban V, signed the decree of his canonization in 1369. The Friars Minor and Conventuals celebrated his feast on 27 September and the Capuchins on 20 October. *The Catholic Encyclopedia*, edited by Charles G. Herbermann (New York, 1913–22), 5:397; Herbert J. Thurston, S. J. and Donald Attwater, eds., *Butler's Lives of the Saints* (New York, 1962), 3:661–62; W. H. Timmons, *El Paso: A Borderlands History* (El Paso, 1990), 56.

3. This is the only retained copy of an original Spanish land grant for San Elizario that has come to light. Copies of a few Spanish-period land grants for San Elizario were recorded in the El Paso County deed books. There is one such example of an even earlier grant, dating from 1798. José María de la Riva to José Estrada, land grant, San Elizario, 2 April 1798, El Paso County Deed Book A, 280–81.

CHAPTER 1

1. John Francis Bannon, *The Spanish Borderlands Frontier, 1513–1821* (New York, 1970), 190–91. For a scholarly, comprehensive study of the Interior Provinces, see Luis Navarro García, *Don José de Gálvez y la Comandancia General de las Provincias Internas del Norte de Nueva España* (Seville, 1964).

2. Max L. Moorhead, *The Presidio: Bastion of the Spanish Borderlands* (Norman, 1975), 56. For Nicolás Lafora's narrative, see Lawrence Kinnaird, ed., *The Frontiers of New Spain* (Berkeley, 1958).

3. Moorhead, *Presidio*, 57–61. For an English translation of the

Royal Regulations of 1772, see Sidney Brinkerhoff and Odie B. Faulk, eds., *Lancers for the King* (Phoenix, 1965).

4. Moorhead, *Presidio*, 68–74. Mark Santiago, *The Red Captain: The Life of Hugo O'Conor, Commandant Inspector of the Interior Provinces of New Spain* (Tucson, 1994), 5.

5. Moorhead, *Presidio*, 75–76.

6. Translated here as mobile company, in Spanish military parlance, *compañía volante* referred to a company with no permanent base of operations. *Diccionario de autoridades* (Madrid, 1979), 3:515; Moorhead, *Presidio*, 80–83.

7. Moorhead, *Presidio*, 84.

8. Ibid., 85–94.

9. Max L. Moorhead, *The Apache Frontier: Jacobo Ugarte and Spanish-Indian Relations in Northern New Spain, 1769–1791* (Norman, 1968), 3.

10. Donald E. Worcester, *The Apaches: Eagles of the Southwest* (Norman, 1979), 4–8; Fernando Jordán, *Crónica de un país bárbaro* (Chihuahua, 1975), 179–80.

11. William B. Griffen, *Utmost Good Faith: Patterns of Apache-Mexican Hostilities In Northern Chihuahua Border Warfare, 1821–1848* (Albuquerque, 1988), 245. See also Daniel S. Matson and Albert H. Schroeder, eds., "Cordero's Description of the Apache— 1796," *New Mexico Historical Review* 32 (October 1957): 337.

12. Matson and Schroeder, "Cordero's Description," 338.

13. Ibid., 339–40.

14. William B. Griffen, *Apaches at War and Peace: The Janos Presidio, 1750–1858* (Albuquerque, 1988), 5–7.

15. John Walton Caughey, *Bernardo de Gálvez In Louisiana, 1776–1783* (Berkeley, 1934), 200–14.

16. Moorhead, *Presidio*, 99.

17. David Weber, *The Spanish Frontier In North America* (New Haven, 1992), 229–30. See also Bernardo de Gálvez, *Instructions for Governing the Interior Provinces of New Spain, 1786*, ed. and trans. by Donald E. Worcester (Berkeley, 1951).

18. Moorhead, *Presidio*, 108–9.

19. Fray Angelico Chavez, *Origins of New Mexico Families: A Genealogy of the Spanish Colonial Period* (Santa Fe, 1992), 82; civil proceeding, Archivo Histórico de Hidalgo del Parral 1645B, 1646A, cited in Gerald J. Mandell, "Commercial Ties Between New Mexico and Parral, 1632 to 1682," 133, ms. in the author's possession.

20. John L. Kessell, Rick Hendricks, and Meredith D. Dodge, eds., *To the Royal Crown Restored: The Journals of don Diego de Vargas, New Mexico, 1692–1694* (Albuquerque, 1995), 75.

21. Tiburcio de Ortega, Statement, AGN, Inquisición 666. Chavez, *Origins*, 246; Mandell, "Commercial Ties," 133.

22. Pablo de Ortega, Statement, AGN, Civil 511; Mandell, "Commercial Ties," 133.

23. John L. Kessell and Rick Hendricks, eds., *By Force of Arms: The Journals of don Diego de Vargas, New Mexico, 1691–1693* (Albuquerque, 1992), 119 n64.

24. Between 1692 and 1712, Tiburcio was the protector of the Indians of the El Paso area, although he was upriver in Santa Fe in 1694. Back in El Paso the following year, Tiburcio served as notary for the Franciscans there. He occupied the positions of councilman and *alguacil mayor* in 1696, but was imprisoned in 1711 for opposing exploitation of the Indians. By 1715 he held the office of alcalde mayor of Jemez, Zia, and Santa Ana Pueblos. Kessell and Hendricks, *By Force of Arms*, 487 n63.

25. Isidro was baptized on 12 April 1682 in El Paso. McLaughlin transcribed Isidro's wife's name as Margarita Peregrina de Aor. Walter V. McLaughlin, Jr., "First Book of Baptisms of Nuestra Señora de Guadalupe del Paso del Norte" (M.A. thesis, University of Texas at El Paso, 1962), 75; Kessell, Hendricks, and Dodge, *To the Royal Crown Restored*, 45.

26. There were two saints named St. Tiburtius, both of whom were beheaded as early Christians. According to legend, a heretic betrayed St. Tiburtius, who was a subdeacon of Rome during the Diocletian persecution, to Roman authorities. To prove his Christian devotion, he walked over burning embers. This miracle was held to be magic, and he was put to death. His day was 14 April. The other St. Tiburtius, traditionally venerated on 11 August, was the brother of Valerius and the betrothed of St. Cecilia, patron saint of music and musicians. Cecilia converted Tiburtius and his brother to Christianity, and they gave themselves over to doing good works. For this, Roman authorities had them executed. This story was popular by the late fifth century. Neither legend is now considered historically accurate. Thurston and Attwater, *Butler's Lives of the Saints*, 2:91, 3:301, 4:402–404; *Catholic Encyclopedia*, 14:720.

27. It is still common usage to form Spanish given names for females from the name of a male saint, such as Micaela from San Miguel. The use of Tiburcio, as opposed to Tiburcia, with both males and females suggests that the given name had become part of the surname Ortega.

28. Plurals of surnames in the eighteenth century still required a plural article, as in Los Lunas (the community in New Mexico), whereas modern usage combines a plural article with a singular form of the surname. Hence, Los Tiburcios was current then, and Los Tiburcio would be expected now.

29. Antonio Padilla and María Antonia Luján, Prenuptial investigation, Las Caldas, 19 August 1739, CAT, r. 2; Diego de Ortega, Criminal proceedings, Los Tiburcios, Senecú, Socorro, and Ysleta, 8–13 January 1770, JA II, r. 9, bk. 2, 1764, f. 55–71, inc.

30. The text quoted here is identified as a verbatim copy of the 1724 document. The long league was defined in the documents Ortega presented as 110 cords of 50 varas each, or 5,500 varas, which was the distance south of Socorro where Ortega's land began. The standard league was 5,000 varas. Mariano Galván Rivera, *Ordenanzas de tierras y aguas o sea formulario geométrico-judicial para la designación, establecimiento, mensura, amojonamiento y deslinde de las poblaciones y todas suertes de tierras, sitios, caballerías y criaderos de ganados mayores y menores y mercedes de aguas* (Mexico City, 1851), 123–29; Francisco Javier Bernal, Investigation, Socorro, 22 October 1802, JA II, r. 14, bk. 1, 1806, f. 468–71; Juan Núñez, Investigation, El Paso, 20 July 1808, JA II, r. 14, bk. 1, 1806, f. 480–83.

31. Galván Rivera, *Ordenanzas de tierras*, 123–29.

32. Rick Hendricks, "Spanish-Indian Relations in El Paso del Norte in the Early Eighteenth Century: The Rebellion of 1711" (Paper read at sixty-first annual meeting of the Society for American Archaeology, New Orleans, 10–14 April 1996); Antonio de Valverde Cosío, Establishment of a capellanía, El Paso, 26 April 1726, JA I, 1774, r. 45, f. 352-60; Rick Hendricks, "Santa María de las Caldas and the

Hacienda de San Antonio: *Diligencias Matrimoniales* from the Lost Curacy, 1733–1739," *Nuestras Raíces* 6:3 (Fall 1994): 117.

33. Benito Crespo, Pastoral visitation, 1729–32, Archives of the Archdiocese of Durango, Book 45.

34. Distribution of tithes from the jurisdiction of El Paso for 1736, El Paso, AHAD–42.

35. Gaspar Domingo de Mendoza, Tabular Report on the Kingdom of New Mexico, Santa Fe, 1739, AGI, México, 1848B; Santiago Torres and Ursula Rosa, Prenuptial investigation, Las Caldas, 2 March 1737, CAT, r. 2; Ventura Cortés and Bárbara, Prenuptial investigation, Las Caldas, 29 August 1737, CAT, r. 4; Antonio Padilla and María Antonia Luján, Prenuptial investigation, Las Caldas, 19 August 1739, CAT, r. 2; Rick Hendricks, "Santa María de las Caldas and the Hacienda de San Antonio: *Diligencias Matrimoniales* from the Lost Curacy, 1733–1739," *Nuestras Raíces* 7:2 (Summer 1995): 77–78; Rick Hendricks, "Santa María de las Caldas and the Hacienda de San Antonio: *Diligencias Matrimoniales* from the Lost Curacy, 1733–1739," *Nuestras Raíces* 7:1 (Spring 1995): 37, 41.

36. Charles Wilson Hackett, ed., *Historical Documents relating to New Mexico, Nueva Vizcaya, and Approaches thereto, to 1773* (Washington, D.C., 1923–27), 3:406–7.

37. Alonso Victores Rubín de Celis to the judges of the treasury of the Cathedral of Durango, Presidio of El Paso, 29 November 1749, AHAD–108, f. 333–34.

38. The terminology applied to the various types of property in the El Paso area is somewhat confusing, but those who lived in the area seem to have used it fairly consistently, the example of Rubín de Celis notwithstanding. A *rancho* was one or more households living on a relatively small farm that produced a variety of crops and engaged in small-scale livestock-raising. A *labor* was typically a farm dedicated to the production of an agricultural crop. *Haciendas* were large, complex operations typically involved in many different activities; they commonly included separate *labores*, often with their own names. The best example from the El Paso area, the Hacienda de San Antonio, included a wheat farm, which bore the name of the hacienda proper; a cattle ranch, Nuestra Señora de Guadalupe; a compound dedicated to pasturing sheep and goats, called Santa Rosa; a workshop for processing wool; and a mill. Hendricks, "Santa María de las Caldas," 6:118. Marc Simmons, "Settlement Patterns and Village Plans in Colonial New Mexico," in *New Spain's Far Northern Frontier: Essays on Spain in the American West, 1540–1821*, David J. Weber, ed. (Albuquerque, 1979), 103–6.

39. Manuel Antonio San Juan to the judge of the treasury of the Cathedral of Durango, Presidio of El Paso, 14 June 1754, AHAD–108, f. 338–40.

40. Donald Cutter, ed., "An Anonymous Statistical Report of Nuevo México in 1765," *New Mexico Historical Review* 50 (October 1975): 347–52; Timmons, *El Paso*, 43; Manuel Antonio San Juan, Certified Copy of the Inspection of the Citizen Militia of El Paso and its Jurisdiction, El Paso, 2–7 July 1762, AGN, Oficio de Soria 5.

41. Antonio María Daroca, El Paso, 24 October 1773, AGN, Provincias Internas 102; Rick Hendricks, "A Documentary History of San Elizario, Texas" in vol. 2, *Lower Valley History*

of *El Valle Bajo: The Culture History of the Lower Rio Grande Valley of El Paso*, John A. Peterson and David O. Brown, eds. (Austin, 1994), 31.

42. Francisco Joaquín Sánchez de Tagle, Land-title registration, El Paso, 2–26 April 1755, JA II, r. 3, bk. 2, 1750, f. 469–568; Juan Tiburcio de Ortega, Land transfer, El Paso, 2 March 1758, JA II, r. 5, bk. 1, 1758, f. 51–54; Diego Varela v. Miguel de Espinosa y Alencaster, Socorro and El Paso, 4 February–10 March 1783, JA II, r. 11, bk. 1, 1783, f. 466–512.

43. Vicente Antonio Archuleta and Juana María Durán, Prenuptial investigation, El Paso, 28 November–5 December 1778, AHAD–29, f. 498–500; Diego Varela vs. Miguel de Espinosa y Alencaster, Socorro and El Paso, 4 February–10 March 1783, JA II, r. 11, bk. 1, 1783, f. 466–512.

44. Lorenzo Antonio Cuarón, Tithe notebook for 1779, El Paso, 24 October 1782, AHAD–135, f. 80–89.

45. Rick Hendricks, "Tabardillo: The 1764 Typhus Epidemic in the El Paso del Norte Area," *Password* 38:2 (Summer 1993): 55–64.

46. Timmons, *El Paso*, 47.

47. Rick Hendricks, *Two Spanish Colonial Censuses of the El Paso Area: 1784 and 1787* (Las Cruces, 1992).

48. Manuel Rengel to Jacobo Ugarte y Loyola, El Paso, 27 April 1787, AGN, Provincias Internas 112; Jacobo Ugarte y Loyola to Manuel Rengel, Arizpe, 18 May 1787, AGN, Provincias Internas 112; Moorhead, *Presidio*, 254–55. Moorhead, *Apache Frontier*, 217–18.

49. Navarro García, *Don José de Gálvez*, 459.

50. Domingo de Ortega to Nemesio Salcedo, San Elizario, 30 September 1807, JA II, r. 14, bk. 1, 1806, f. 475–77.

51. The documents that detail these events are later copies. In them, Ortega, who stated that he was one hundred years old at the time (1807), indicated that the events in question occurred in 1782. Either he was mistaken about the date or there was a scribal error made when these copies were generated. There is little doubt that the decision to abandon Los Tiburcios was reached in 1787.

52. Navarro García, *Don José de Gálvez*, 492; Moorhead, *Presidio*, 90.

53. José María to Francisco Javier de Uranga, Senecú, 23 August 1788, JA I, r. 47, 1788, f. 117; Marcos Guerra to Francisco Javier de Uranga, Senecú, 29 August 1788, JA I, r. 47, 1788, f. 116.

54. The noted Spanish historian, Luis Navarro García, citing sources from the Archivo General de Indias in Seville, gave 1789 as the year of the relocation of San Elizario. *Don José de Gálvez*, 492. Eugene O. Porter misread the removal order and used 1780. *San Elizario: A History* (Austin, 1973), 37–38. W. H. Timmons corrected Porter's error in "The Presidio of San Elizario, 1789–1851," *Password* 33:3 (Fall 1988): 107. Diego de Borica to Francisco Javier de Uranga, Chihuahua, 14 February 1789, JA I, r. 1, 1788, bk. 6, f. 188– 90.

55. Moorhead, *Presidio*, 166–67. Rex E. Gerald, *Spanish Presidios of the Late Eighteenth Century in Northern New Spain* (Santa Fe, 1968), 14–15, 24, [33].

56. *Plan of the Mexican Presidio at San Elizario, Texas, 1847*. For a detailed survey of presidial architecture see Jack Stephen Williams, "Architecture and Defense on the Military Frontier of Arizona, 1752–1856" (Ph.D. diss., University of Ari-

zona, 1991).

57. Roscoe P. Conkling and Margaret B. Conkling, *The Butterfield Overland Mail, 1875–1869* (Glendale, 1947), 3:51–52. The Conklings' observations are quoted in Timmons, "Presidio of San Elizario," 112 and on page 64 above.

58. Gerald, *Spanish Presidios*, 26.

59. Moorhead, *Presidio*, 169.

60. *Plan of the Mexican Presidio at San Elizario, Texas, 1847.*

61. Gerald, *Spanish Presidios*, 16.

62. Receipt for the Indians of Socorro, San Elizario, 26 April 1789, JA I, 1798, r. 48.

63. Francisco Martínez to Francisco Javier de Uranga, San Elizario, 16 June 1789, JA II, r. 11, 1784, bk. 1, f. 56–58.

64. Antonio de Arce to Francisco Javier de Uranga, San Elizario, 18 May 1790, JA I, r. 47, 1790, f. 37; Antonio de Arce to Francisco Javier de Uranga, San Elizario, 21 June 1790, JA I, r. 47, 1790, f. 39.

65. Antonio Cordero, Inspection report, San Elizario, 13 May 1790, AGS, Guerra Moderna 7047:52.

66. Pedro de Nava to Francisco Javier de Uranga, Chihuahua, 7 November 1791, JA I, r. 47, 1790, f. 302.

67. Pedro de Nava to the lieutenant governor of El Paso, Order, 7 January 1793, JA I, r. 47, 1791, f. 217; Marcos [illegible] to Francisco Javier de Uranga, San Elizario, 8 January 1793, JA I, r. 47, 1791, f. 344–45.

68. Pedro de Nava to Francisco Javier de Uranga, Chihuahua, 1 February 1793, JA I, 1791, r. 47, f. 229–30.

69. Manuel Vidal de Lorca to Francisco Javier de Uranga, San Elizario, 21 February 1793, JA I, r. 47, 1793, f. 256–57.

70. This Antonio Cordero was a local resident of the El Paso area and is not to be confused with the officer of the same name. Hendricks, *Two Spanish Colonial Censuses*, 22.

71. Manuel Vidal de Lorca to Francisco Javier de Uranga, San Elizario, 9 March 1793, JA I, r. 47, 1793, f. 268; Manuel Vidal de Lorca to Francisco Javier de Uranga, San Elizario, 13 March 1793, JA I, r. 47, 1793, f. 264; Manuel Vidal de Lorca to Francisco Javier de Uranga, San Elizario, 16 March 1793, JA I, r. 47, 1793, f. 262.

72. Manuel Vidal de Lorca to Francisco Javier de Uranga, San Elizario, 27 April 1793, JA I, r. 47, 1793, f. 288.

73. Pedro de Nava to the conde del Campo de Alange, Chihuahua, 1 August 1793, AGI, Guadalajara 289.

74. Rick Hendricks, "Massacre in the Organ Mountains: The Death of Manuel Vidal de Lorca," *Password* 39:4 (Winter 1994): 174.

75. Pedro de Nava to the lieutenant governor of El Paso, Chihuahua, 18 December 1794, JA II, r. 13A, bk. 1, 1794, f. 129.

76. Joaquín Velarde to the commandant of San Elizario, 5 June 1841, JA II, r. 32, 1841, bk. 3, f. 343; Joaquín Velarde to the commandant of San Elizario, 17 June 1841, JA II, r. 32, 1841, bk. 3, f. 349.

CHAPTER 2

1. John L. Kessell, *Friars, Soldiers, and Reformers: Hispanic Arizona and the Sonora Mission Frontier, 1767–1856* (Tucson, 1976), 163.

2. Moorhead, *Presidio*, 101; Worcester, *Instructions*, 87–146.

3. Griffen points out that Apache rancherias as recorded in

Spanish and Mexican records were administrative units and that it is uncertain how they corresponded to individual groups as the Apaches themselves understood them. William B. Griffen, "The Chiracahua Apache Population Resident at the Janos Presidio, 1792–1858," *Journal of the Southwest* 33 (Summer 1991): 157.

4. Manuel Rengel to Jacobo Ugarte y Loyola, El Paso, 27 April 1787, AGN, Provincias Internas 112; Moorhead, *Presidio*, 254–55.

5. Jacobo Ugarte y Loyola to Manuel Rengel, Arizpe, 18 May 1787, AGN, Provincias Internas 112.

6. Navarro García, *Don José de Gálvez*, 459.

7. Moorhead, *Presidio*, 254.

8. Alberto Máynez, Transmittal of an order, El Paso, 14 July 1787, JA II, r. 12, bk. 1, 1787, f. 3–4.

9. Navarro García, *Don José de Gálvez*, 492; Moorhead, *Presidio*, 90. Timmons, "Presidio of San Elizario," 107–15; Diego de Borica to Francisco Javier de Uranga, Chihuahua, 14 February 1789, JA I, r. 1, bk. 6, 1788, f. 188–90.

10. Antonio Cordero, Extract of an inspection, San Elizario, 13 May 1790, AGS, Guerra Moderna 7047:52.

11. Moorhead identifies these individuals as Mescaleros. As Griffen has observed, Spanish documents reflect their cultural biases with respect to the Apaches. Hence, the Spaniards relied on the norms of their own male-dominated, class-stratified conception of society even though Apache society was characterized by "small, egalitarian social units (rancherias), with no political bureaucracy, and where family and kinship were the only important relationships." (Griffen, "Chiracahua Apache Population," 158.)

The identification of these individuals and the groups they were associated with is problematic. Of the twenty-five men whose names Spaniards attempted to transliterate from Apache to Spanish and who are identified as Apache leaders in Juárez Archive documents, fewer than half can be identified with certainty, largely because they appear in the work of Moorhead and Griffen and can therefore be corroborated. Inquiries among Mescalero Apache informants conducted in 1995 by Scott Rushforth, chairman of the Department of Sociology and Anthropology at New Mexico State University and an Athapaskan linguist, failed to establish any links with present-day Apache family groups. (Scott Rushforth, Personal communication, Las Cruces, New Mexico, January 1995; Moorhead, *Apache Frontier*, 202, 218.)

12. Francisco Javier de Uranga to Jacobo Ugarte y Loyola, El Paso, 17 February 1790, AGN, Provincias Internas 66.

13. Jacobo Ugarte y Loyola to Francisco Javier de Uranga, Chihuahua, 22 February 1790, JA II, r. 13, bk. 1, 1790, f. 107–9; Diego de Borica to Francisco Javier de Uranga, Chihuahua, 15 March 1790, JA II, r. 13, bk. 1, 1790, f. 101.

14. Jacobo Ugarte y Loyola to Francisco Javier de Uranga, Chihuahua, 28 March 1790, JA II, r. 13, bk. 1, 1790, f. 98–100; Extractos del expediente sobre gastos para las paces con los indios apaches de Nueva Vizcaya, 9 March 1790, AGN, Provincias Internas 65.

15. Jacobo Ugarte y Loyola to Francisco Javier de Uranga, Chihuahua, 8 June 1790, JA II, r. 13, bk. 1, 1790, f. 115–16.

16. Jacobo Ugarte y Loyola to Francisco Javier de Uranga, Chihuahua, 19 June 1790, JA II, r. 13, bk. 1, 1790, f. 110–11.

17. Nicolás Villaroel, Declaration, Presidio of El Norte, [June] 1792, AGN, Provincias Internas 170.

18. Extractos del expediente sobre gastos para las paces con los indios Apaches de Nueva Vizcaya, 11 June 1790, AGN, Provincias Internas 65.

19. Jacobo Ugarte y Loyola to Francisco Javier de Uranga, Chihuahua, 30 July 1790, JA II, r. 13, bk. 1, 1790, f. 124–25.

20. The repeated unsuccessful attempts to get Capitancillo Barrio to settle at San Elizario figure prominently in the correspondence for 1793 and 1794. For example, see Manuel Vidal de Lorca to Francisco Javier de Uranga, San Elizario, 23 March 1793, JA II, r. 13A, bk. 1, 1791, f. 230; Manuel Vidal de Lorca to Francisco Javier de Uranga, San Elizario, 16 June 1793, JA II, r. 13A, bk. 1, 1791, f. 264; Manuel Vidal de Lorca to the lieutenant governor of El Paso, San Elizario, 22 November 1793, JA II, r. 13A, bk. 1, 1791, f. 85–86. In early 1794 Barrio abandoned the El Paso area and by 1795 had apparently opted for open warfare against the Spaniards. Manuel Vidal de Lorca to Francisco Javier de Uranga, San Elizario, 9 March 1794, JA II, r. 13, bk. 1, 1794, f. 84– 85, 87–88; Antonio Cordero to Francisco Javier de Uranga, Chihuahua, 26 February 1795, JA I, 1790, r. 47, f. 273.

21. Jacobo Ugarte y Loyola to Francisco Javier de Uranga, Chihuahua, 21 August 1790, JA II, r. 13, bk. 1, 1790, f. 131.

22. Antonio Cordero to Francisco Javier de Uranga, Chihuahua, 9 September 1790, JA II, r. 13, bk. 1, 1790, f. 135–36.

23. Antonio Cordero to Francisco Javier de Uranga, Chihuahua, 9 September 1790, JA II, r. 13, bk. 1, 1790, f. 137.

24. Antonio Cordero to Francisco Javier de Uranga, Chihuahua, 6 October 1790, JA II, r. 13, bk. 1, 1790, f. 134.

25. Antonio Cordero to Francisco Javier de Uranga, Chihuahua, 17 January 1791, JA II, r. 13, bk. 1, 1790, f. 480; Antonio Cordero to the lieutenant governor of El Paso, Chihuahua, 4 February 1791, JA II, r. 13, bk. 1, 1790, f. 482–83.

26. Antonio Cordero to Francisco Javier de Uranga, Chihuahua, 8 February 1791, JA II, r. 13, bk. 1, 1790, f. 485–87.

27. Juan Francisco Granados to Antonio Cordero, Chihuahua, 15 February 1791, JA II, r. 13, bk. 1, 1790, f. 491–92; Antonio Cordero to Francisco Javier de Uranga, Chihuahua, 15 February 1791, JA II, r. 13, bk. 1, 1790, f. 493; Antonio Cordero to Francisco Javier de Uranga, Chihuahua, 25 February 1791, JA II, r. 13, bk. 1, 1790, f. 489.

28. Antonio Cordero to Francisco Javier de Uranga, Chihuahua, 25 February 1791, JA II, r. 13, bk. 1, 1790, f. 488.

29. Antonio Cordero to Francisco Javier de Uranga, Chihuahua, 11 March 1791, JA II, r. 13, bk. 1, 1790, f. 494.

30. Antonio Cordero to the lieutenant governor of El Paso, Chihuahua, 6 April 1791, JA II, r. 13, bk. 1, 1790, f. 495–96.

31. The Apache leader known to the Spaniards as Mallá (or Mayá) is not to be confused with the Comanche leader, Ecueracapa, also known as Malla. Noticia de los capitanes comanches presentada en la villa de Santa Fe y pueblo de Pecos, AGN, Provincias Internas 65; Alfred Barnaby Thomas, *Forgotten Frontiers: A Study of the Spanish Indian Policy of Don Juan Bautista de Anza, Governor of New Mexico, 1777–1787* (Norman, 1969), 325; Antonio Cordero to Francisco Javier de Uranga, 8 April 1791, JA II, r. 13, bk. 1, 1790, f. 506–7.

32. This situation appears remarkably similar to the one Kessell

described in Sonora in the 1790s. He writes that "the Apache peace was a relative thing, at worst a sham. When it suited their purposes to raid and kill, some of them still did." (Kessell, *Friars, Soldiers, and Reformers*, 201; Fernando de la Concha to Francisco Javier de Uranga, Santa Fe, 20 April 1791, JA II, r. 13, bk. 1, 1791, f. 123.)

33. Antonio Cordero to Francisco Javier de Uranga, 1 May 1791, JA II, r. 13, bk. 1, 1790, f. 508.

34. Francisco Javier Bernal to Fernando de la Concha, El Paso, 30 May 1791, SANM II:1124.

35. Antonio Cordero to Francisco Javier de Uranga, 9 May 1791, JA II, r. 13, bk. 1, 1790, f. 509.

36. Antonio Cordero to the lieutenant governor of El Paso, Chihuahua, 8 May 1791, JA II, r. 13, bk. 1, 1790, f. 510.

37. Antonio Cordero to the lieutenant governor of El Paso, Namiquipa, 9 July 1791, JA II, r. 13, bk. 1, 1790, f. 515.

38. Antonio Cordero to the lieutenant governor of El Paso, Janos, 19 July 1791, JA II, r. 13, bk. 1, 1790, f. 516–17; Pedro de Nava to the lieutenant governor of El Paso, Chihuahua, ? July 1791, JA II, r. 13, bk. 1, 1788, f. 364.

39. There is nothing in the documentary record to suggest that Apaches participating in the peace program at San Elizario built buildings and established farms, although ongoing archaeological investigations may yet determine that they did. Such was the case in the Big Bend area, which proved to be a key area for experimentation with the peace program because of the apparent receptiveness of the Mescaleros. (Elizabeth A. H. John. "Spanish-Indian Relations in the Big Bend Region during the Eighteenth and Early Nineteenth Centuries," *The Journal of Big Bend Studies*

3 (January 1991): 74–79; Francisco Javier de Uranga, Report, El Paso, 30 September 1792, AGN, Provincias Internas 193–1; Francisco Javier de Uranga, Report, El Paso, 31 October 1792, AGN, Provincias Internas 193–1.)

40. Antonio Cordero to the lieutenant governor of El Paso, El Paso, 12 August 1791, JA II, r. 13, bk. 1, 1790, f. 523.

41. Antonio Cordero to the lieutenant governor of El Paso, El Paso, 12 August 1791, JA II, r. 13, bk. 1, 1790, f. 524.

42. Antonio Cordero to the lieutenant governor of El Paso, El Paso, 14 August 1791, JA II, r. 13, bk. 1, 1790, f. 522.

43. Pedro de Nava to the lieutenant governor of El Paso, Chihuahua, 19 August 1791, JA II, r. 13, bk. 1, 1788, f. 323.

44. Manuel Rengel to the lieutenant governor of El Paso, [Carrizal], 3 September 1791, JA II, r. 13, bk. 1, 1791, f. 119–20.

45. Jasquenelté was usually identified as a mimbreño, or Mimbres Apache. According to Griffen, the Chiricahuas, or Southern Apaches, were referred to in Spanish documents as Chiricaguis, Gileños, Mimbreños, and Mogolloneros. (Griffen, "Chiracahua Apache Population," 160.)

46. Jacobo Ugarte y Loyola to the Conde de Revillagigedo, Hacienda del Carmen, 19 May 1790, AGN, Provincias Internas 66.

47. Manuel Merino to Francisco Javier de Uranga, Chihuahua, 27 July 1791, SANM II:1138.

48. Antonio de Arce and Juan Antonio de Arce to Pedro de Nava, Account of expenses for Apaches at peace from 1 April to 26 June 1791, San Elizario, 26 June 1791, AGN, Provincias Internas 66.

49. Diego de Borica to the lieutenant governor of El Paso,

Chihuahua, 8 July 1791, r. 13, bk. 1, 1790, f. 518–19; Pedro de Nava to Francisco Javier de Uranga, Chihuahua, 10 October 1791, r. 13, bk. 1, 1788, f. 397.

50. Moorhead summarized and analyzed Nava's instructions, but failed to discuss fully one third of its articles. Griffen also included a brief discussion of Nava's instructions. Because of the importance of this document to the history of the Apache peace establishment at the presidio of San Elizario, a complete translation is included in the documentary appendix. Copies of Nava's original are in the JA II and the AGI. (Pedro de Nava, Instructions for dealing with the Apaches at peace in Nueva Vizcaya, Chihuahua, 14 October 1791, JA II, r. 13, bk. 1, 1788, f. 325–49; Pedro de Nava, Instructions for dealing with the Apaches at peace in Nueva Vizcaya, Chihuahua, 14 October 1791, AGI, Guadalajara 289. Moorhead, *Presidio*, 261–65; Griffen, *Apaches*, 99–100.)

51. Jack S. Williams, Pedro de Nava's Instructions for Governing the Apache Establishments of Peace, 1791, unpublished ms. in the author's possession, (Tucson, 1985).

52. Moorhead, *Presidio*, 261–65.

53. Pedro de Nava to the lieutenant governor of El Paso, Chihuahua, 10 October 1791, JA II, r. 13, bk. 1, 1788, f. 398.

54. Pedro de Nava to the lieutenant governor of El Paso, Chihuahua, 8 November 1791, JA II, r. 13, bk. 1, 1790, f. 525–26.

55. Pedro de Nava to the lieutenant governor of El Paso, Chihuahua, 8 November 1791, JA II, r. 13, bk. 1, 1790, f. 528.

56. Pedro de Nava to the lieutenant governor of El Paso, Chihuahua, 7 February 1792, JA II, r. 13, bk. 1, 1788, f. 393.

57. Pedro de Nava to Francisco Javier de Uranga, Chihuahua, 31 March 1792, JA II, r. 13, bk. 1, 1788, f. 385.

58. Pedro de Nava to Francisco Javier de Uranga, Chihuahua, 7 April 1792, JA II, r. 13, bk. 1, 1788, f. 386. For more information on eighteenth-century epidemic disease in the El Paso area, see Hendricks, "Tabardillo," 55–64.

59. Pedro de Nava to Antonio Cordero, Chihuahua, 29 May 1792, AGN, Provincias Internas 170; Francisco Javier Bernal, Declaration, El Paso, 13 July 1792, AGN, Provincias Internas 170; Juan Pedro Rivera, Declaration, El Paso, 13 July 1792, AGN, Provincias Internas 170.

60. Pedro de Nava to Francisco Javier de Uranga, Chihuahua, 7 April 1792, JA II, r. 13, bk. 1, 1788, f. 387–88; Pedro de Nava to the lieutenant governor of El Paso, San Diego, ? May 1792, JA II, r. 13, bk. 1, 1788, f. 383–84.

61. Pedro de Nava to the lieutenant governor of El Paso, Chihuahua, ? Ju? 1792, JA II, r. 13, bk. 1, 1788, f. 381–82; Pedro de Nava to Francisco Javier de Uranga, Chihuahua, 25 July 1792, JA II, r. 13, bk. 1, 1788, f. 378.

62. Pedro de Nava to the lieutenant governor of El Paso, Chihuahua, 25 July 1792, JA II, r. 13, bk. 1, 1788, f. 375–76.

63. Pedro de Nava to Francisco Javier de Uranga, Chihuahua, 6 August 1792, JA II, r. 13, bk. 1, 1788, f. 377; Pedro de Nava to the lieutenant governor of El Paso, Chihuahua, 14 September 1792, JA II, r. 13, bk. 1, 1788, f. 371.

64. Pedro de Nava to Francisco Javier de Uranga, Chihuahua, 25 July 1792, JA II, r. 13, bk. 1, 1788, f. 378.

65. Diego de Borica to Francisco Javier de Uranga, Chihuahua, 8 December 1792, JA II, r. 13, bk. 1, 1788, f. 369.

66. Pedro de Nava to Francisco Javier de Uranga, Chihuahua, 1

February 1793, JA II, r. 13A, bk. 1, 1791, f. 174–76.

67. Manuel Vidal de Lorca to Francisco Javier de Uranga, San Elizario, 2 April 1793, JA II, r. 13A, bk. 1, 1791, f. 250–52.

68. Manuel Vidal de Lorca to Francisco Javier de Uranga, San Elizario, 28 July 1793, JA II, r. 13A, bk. 1, 1791, f. 69–70.

69. Pablo Sandoval to Francisco Javier de Uranga, Alamitos, 12–13 August 1793, JA II, r. 13, bk. 1, 1791, f. 7–10.

70. Manuel Vidal de Lorca to Francisco Javier de Uranga, San Elizario, 14 September 1793, JA II, r. 13A, bk. 1, 1791, f. 238.

71. Manuel Vidal de Lorca to the lieutenant governor of El Paso, San Elizario, [5 December 1793], JA II, r. 13A, bk. 1, 1791, f. 176–78; Pedro de Nava to Francisco Javier de Uranga, Chihuahua, 7 January 1794, JA II, r. 13A, bk. 1, 1794, f. 95.

72. Manuel Vidal de Lorca to the lieutenant governor of El Paso, San Elizario, 14 January 1794, JA II, r. 13A, bk. 1, 1794, f. 75–76; Francisco Javier de Uranga to Manuel Vidal de Lorca, El Paso, 16 January 1794, JA II, r. 13A, bk. 1, 1794, f. 74; Manuel Vidal de Lorca to the lieutenant governor of El Paso, San Elizario, 16 January 1794, JA II, r. 13A, bk. 1, 1794, f. 72–73.

73. Manuel Vidal de Lorca to the lieutenant governor of El Paso, San Elizario, 6 February 1794, JA II, r. 13A, bk. 1, 1794, f. 70–71.

74. Manuel Vidal de Lorca to the lieutenant governor of El Paso, San Elizario, 23 February 1794, JA II, r. 13A, bk. 1, 1794, f. 58–59.

75. Manuel Vidal de Lorca to Francisco Javier de Uranga, San Elizario, 3 March 1794, JA II, r. 13A, bk. 1, 1794, f. 82.

76. Manuel Vidal de Lorca to Francisco Javier de Uranga, San Elizario, 8 March 1794, JA II, r. 13A, bk. 1, 1794, f. 40–41.

77. Navarro García, *Don José de Gálvez*, 492.

78. Manuel Rengel to Francisco Javier de Uranga, San Elizario, 17 April 1794, JA II, r. 13A, bk. 1, 1794, f. 207–8.

79. Manuel Rengel to Francisco Javier de Uranga, San Elizario, 19 April 1794, JA II, r. 13A, bk. 1, 1794, f. 36–39.

80. José Escageda to the justicias of Socorro, Ysleta, the real of San Lorenzo, and El Paso, San Elizario, 25 May 1794, JA II, r. 13A, bk. 1, 1794, f. 161; Antonio Arroy to Francisco Javier de Uranga, San Elizario, 25 May 1794, JA II, r. 13A, bk. 1, 1794, f. 162; Francisco Javier de Uranga, Edict, El Paso, 16 June 1794, JA II, r. 13A, bk. 1, 1794, f. 189–90; José Escageda to the lieutenant governor of El Paso, San Elizario, 19 June 1794, JA II, r. 13A, bk. 1, 1794, f. 145; Pedro de Nava to Francisco Javier de Uranga, Chihuahua, 23 June 1794, JA II, r. 13A, bk. 1, 1794, f. 103–4.

81. Manuel Rengel to Francisco Javier de Uranga, Fray Cristóbal, 14 June 1794, JA II, r. 13A, bk. 1, 1794, f. 200–201.

82. Pedro de Nava to the lieutenant governor of El Paso, Chihuahua, 11 July 1794, JA II, r. 13A, bk. 1, 1794, f. 108–9.

83. José de Escageda to the lieutenant governor of El Paso, San Elizario, 4 August 1794, JA II, r. 13A, bk. 1, 1794, f. 153.

84. Francisco Javier de Uranga to Pedro de Nava, El Paso, 4 October 1794, JA II, r. 13A, bk. 1, 1794, f. 192.

85. Antonio Vargas to Francisco Javier de Uranga, San Elizario, 30 May 1795, JA II, r. 13A, bk. 1, 1794, f. 402–3; Francisco Javier de Uranga, Edict, El Paso, 1 June 1795, JA I, 1794, r. 48, f. 258–59.

86. Antonio Vargas to the lieutenant governor of El Paso, San

Elizario, 8 August 1795, JA II, r. 13A, bk. 1, 1794, f. 418–19.

87. Manuel Rengel to Francisco Javier de Uranga, San Elizario, 10 April 1797, JA II, 1798, r. 13A, bk. 1, 1798, f. 118; Manuel Rengel to Francisco Javier Bernal, Los Tiburcios, 8 May 1797 JA II, r. 13A, bk. 1, 1798, f. 117.

88. José María de la Riva to Francisco Javier de Uranga, San Elizario, 18 July 1797, JA II, r. 13A, bk. 1, 1798, f. 107–9.

89. Manuel Rengel to Francisco Javier de Uranga, Los Tiburcios, 1 August 1797, JA II, r. 13A, bk. 1, 1798, f. 120.

90. Griffen identifies Chafalote as a Gileño (Mimbreño) Apache. (Griffen, *Apaches*, 39.)

91. Pedro de Nava to Miguel Cañuelas, Chihuahua, 9 August 1798, JA II, r. 14, bk. 1, 1798, f. 16–17; Pedro de Nava to the lieutenant governor of El Paso, Chihuahua, 12 December 1798, JA II, r. 14, bk. 1, 1798, f. 11–14.

92. José María de la Riva to lieutenant governor of El Paso, San Elizario, 14 November 1798, JA II, r. 14, bk. 1, 1798, f. 19–20.

93. Fernando Chacón to Pedro de Nava, Santa Fe, 18 November 1798, SANM II:1430; Cited in J. Richard Salazar, "Spanish-Indian Relations in New Mexico During the Term of Commandant General Pedro de Nava, 1790–1802" (Guadalupita, N. Mex., 1994), 20.

94. Pedro de Nava to Manuel Merino, Chihuahua, 13 March 1799, SANM II:1444.

95. Pedro de Nava to the governor of New Mexico, Chihuahua, 14 September 1799, SANM II:1463.

96. Fernando Chacón to Pedro de Nava, El Paso, 29 August 1800, SANM II:1502.

97. See, for example, Fernando Chacón to Pedro de Nava,

Journal, Santa Fe, 1 April 1801, SANM II:1548; Fernando Chacón to Pedro de Nava, Santa Fe, 29 August 1801, SANM II:1563; Joaquín del Real Alencaster to Nemesio Salcedo, Santa Fe, 15 May 1805, SANM II:1828.

98. Fernando Chacón, Journal, Santa Fe, 3 March 1804, SANM II:1715.

99. José Manrrique was governor of New Mexico from 1808 to 1814. (Thomas C. Barnes, Thomas H. Naylor, and Charles W. Polzer, *Northern New Spain: A Research Guide* (Tucson, 1981), 105.)

100. José Manrrique to the lieutenant governor of El Paso, San Elizario, 16 April 1806, JA II, r. 14, bk. 1, 1806, f. 91.

101. José Manrrique to the lieutenant governor of El Paso, San Elizario, ? April 1806, JA II, r. 14, bk. 1, 1806, f. 92.

102. José Manrrique to the lieutenant governor of El Paso, San Elizario, 19 May 1806, JA II, r. 14, bk. 1, 1806, f. 85–86.

103. Nemesio Salcedo to José Manrrique, San Diego, 17 May 1808, SANM II:2104.

104. José Manrrique to the lieutenant governor of El Paso, San Elizario, 19 May 1806, JA II, r. 14, bk. 1, 1806, f. 85–86.

105. José Manrrique to the lieutenant governor of El Paso, San Elizario, 7 June 1806, JA II, r. 14, bk. 1, 1806, f. 81.

106. José Manrrique to the lieutenant governor of El Paso, San Elizario, 20 August 1806, JA II, r. 14, bk. 1, 1806, f. 61; José Manrrique to the lieutenant governor of El Paso, San Elizario, 22 August 1806, JA II, r. 14, bk. 1, 1806, f. 62; José Manrrique to the lieutenant governor of El Paso, San Elizario, 3 September 1806, JA II, r. 14, bk. 1, 1806, f. 46; José Manrrique to Isidro Rey, San Elizario, 28 September 1806, JA II, r. 14, bk. 1, 1806, f. 50.

107. José Manrrique to the lieutenant governor of El Paso, San Elizario, 30 August 1806, JA II, r. 14, bk. 1, 1806, f. 58.

108. José Manrrique to the lieutenant governor of El Paso, San Elizario, 20 November 1806, JA II, r. 14, bk. 1, 1806, f. 52; José Manrrique to the lieutenant governor of El Paso, San Elizario, 26 November 1806, JA II, r. 14, bk. 1, 1806, f. 54.

109. José Manrrique to the lieutenant governor of El Paso, San Elizario, 2? November 1806, JA II, r. 14, bk. 1, 1806, f. 56–57.

110. José Manrrique to the lieutenant governor of El Paso, San Elizario, 20 December 1806, JA II, r. 14, bk. 1, 1806, f. 55.

111. José Manrrique to Isidro Rey, San Elizario, 10 January 1807, JA II, r. 14, bk. 1, 1806, f. 362.

112. Jacobo Ugarte y Loyola named Alberto Máynez to replace Francisco Javier Bernal as lieutenant governor at El Paso in early January 1787. The following year, Ugarte y Loyola complied with Máynez's request for a military posting and named Francisco Javier de Uranga as his successor. Máynez served as interim governor of New Mexico in 1808 and then again from 1808 to 1814. (Barnes, Naylor, and Polzer, *Northern New Spain*, 105. Jacobo Ugarte y Loyola to Francisco Javier Bernal, Chihuahua, 2 January 1787, JA II, r. 12, bk. 1, 1787, f. 33; Jacobo Ugarte y Loyola to the citizens of the El Paso jurisdiction, Arizpe, 5 January 1788, JA II, r. 13, bk. 1, 1788, f. 108–9.)

113. José Manrrique to Isidro Rey, San Elizario, 28 January 1807, JA II, r. 14, bk. 1, 1806, f. 364; José Manrrique to Isidro Rey, San Elizario, 29 January 1807, JA II, r. 14, bk. 1, 1806, f. 365.

114. José Manrrique to Isidro Rey, San Elizario, 3 March 1807,

JA II, r. 14, bk. 1, 1806, f. 366.

115. For example, see José Manrrique to Isidro Rey, San Elizario, 25 April 1807, JA II, r. 14, bk. 1, 1806, f. 367; José Manrrique to Isidro Rey, San Elizario, 12 May 1807, JA II, r. 14, bk. 1, 1806, f. 368; Nicolás Tarín to Isidro Rey, San Elizario, 16 June 1807, JA II, r. 14, bk. 1, 1806, f. 372.

116. Nicolás Tarín to the lieutenant governor of El Paso, San Elizario, 26 October 1807, JA II, r. 14, bk. 1, 1806, f. 399.

117. Nicolás Tarín to the lieutenant governor of El Paso, San Elizario, 28 October 1807, JA II, r. 14, bk. 1, 1806, f. 400–401.

118. Nicolás Tarín to the lieutenant governor of El Paso, San Elizario, 11 November 1807, JA II, r. 14, bk. 1, 1806, f. 405.

119. José Manrrique to Isidro Rey, San Elizario, 27 November 1807, JA II, r. 14, bk. 1, 1806, f. 406.

120. Nemesio Salcedo to the lieutenant governor of El Paso, Chihuahua, 5 March 1808, JA II, r. 15, bk. 1, 1806, f. 57–58.

121. Nemesio Salcedo to the lieutenant governor of El Paso, Chihuahua, 3 August 1808, JA II, r. 15, bk. 1, 1806, f. 64.

122. Nemesio Salcedo to José Manrrique, San Diego, 17 May 1808, SANM II:2104; José Joaquín Ugarte to the governor of New Mexico, San Elizario, 18 August 1801, SANM II:1618.

123. Manuel Ignacio de Arvizu, Report, San Elizario, 13 February 1809, SANM II:2203.

124. José Manuel de Ochoa to Isidro Rey, San Elizario, 5 April 1809, JA II, r. 15, bk. 1, 1806, f. 187, 189; José Manuel de Ochoa to Isidro Rey, San Elizario, 29 April 1809, JA II, r. 15, bk. 1, 1806, f. 188; José Manuel de Ochoa to Isidro Rey, San

Elizario, 30 April 1809, JA II, r. 15, bk. 1, 1806, f. 185–86; Félix Colomo to Isidro Rey, San Elizario, 2 June 1809, JA II, r. 15, bk. 1, 1806, f. 183–84.

125. Félix Colomo to Isidro Rey, San Elizario, 3 June 1809, JA II, r. 15, bk. 1, 1806, f. 181–82.

126. Juan Francisco Granados to Isidro Rey, San Elizario, 20 June 1809, JA II, r. 15, bk. 1, 1806, f. 179; Juan Francisco Granados to Isidro Rey, San Elizario, 15 September 1809, JA II, r. 15, bk. 1, 1806, f. 190–91.

127. Pedro Baptista Pino, *The Exposition on the Province of New Mexico, 1812*, trans. and ed. with an introduction by Adrian Bustamante and Marc Simmons (Albuquerque, 1995), 18.

128. Timmons, *El Paso*, 60.

129. Isidro Rey to Joaquín del Real Alencaster, El Paso, 31 August 1806, SANM II:2009; José Manrrique to Isidro Rey, San Elizario, 23 August 1807, JA II, r. 14, bk 1, 1806, frame 386.

130. Donald Jackson, ed., *The Journal of Zebulon Pike* (Norman, 1966), 1:409–10; Timmons, "Presidio of San Elizario," 108–9; Timmons, *El Paso*, 59.

131. Nemesio Salcedo to the interim governor of New Mexico, Chihuahua, 14 May 1810, SANM II:2321.

132. Timmons, "Presidio of San Elizario," 109.

133. Timmons, *El Paso*, 63.

134. Simón Elías González, List of the individuals from the presidio of San Elizario present for the publication the Spanish Constitution, Chihuahua, 30 October 1813, AGN, Caja Matriz.

135. Libro manual de la Real Caja de Chihuahua del cargo del ministro de la real hacienda, contador y tesorero de ella don Diego de Aguirre y Rosales para la cuenta del año de 1816 (Disbursements for 1 July, 3 October, and 11 December) AGN, Caja Matriz, Acervo 82, Caja 1352.

136. Isidro Rey to the interim lieutenant governor of New Mexico, San Elizario, 30 August 1815, SANM II:2623; Juan Cáceres, Receipts for supplies from San Elizario detachment in New Mexico, Albuquerque, 3 November 1818, SANM II:2767; Rick Hendricks, "A Muster of the Presidio of San Elizario in 1819," *Password* 39:3 (Fall 1994): 136–39.

137. Timmons, "Presidio of San Elizario," 110.

138. Max L. Moorhead, *New Mexico's Royal Road* (Norman, 1958), 59

139. Juan Cáceres, Receipts for supplies from San Elizario detachment in New Mexico, Albuquerque, 3 November 1818, SANM II:2767; José Montoya, Accounting of beans and chile for presidios, Jemez, 22 May 1819, SANM II:2821.

140. Alejo García Conde to Facundo Melgares, Durango, 4 December 1819, SANM II:2863.

141. Griffen reported similar observations for Janos presidio from which it is assumed that the same process took place at San Elizario. (Griffen, "Chiracahua Apache Population," 153– 55.)

142. Alberto Máynez, Report, Santa Fe, 12 July 1815, SANM II:2607; Isidro Rey to the lieutenant governor of New Mexico, San Elizario, 18 September 1815, SANM II:2623. Griffen, *Apaches*, 89.

143. Alejo García Conde to Facundo Melgares, Durango, 4 December 1819, SANM II:2863.

144. Instructions for selection of deputies to the Spanish Cortes,

Durango, 5 July 1820, SANM II:2903.

145. Timmons, "Presidio of San Elizario," 110; Timmons, *El Paso*, 72.

CHAPTER 3

1. W. H. Timmons, "The El Paso Area in the Mexican Period, 1821–1848," *Southwestern Historical Quarterly* 84 (July 1980): 3; Francisco R. Almada, *Resumen de historia del Estado de Chihuahua* (n.p., 1986), 181–82.

2. Marcelino Escageda, Decree, Puesto of San Elizario, 9 December 1823, El Paso County Deed Book A, 217; Juan Carrasco to José Ignacio Ronquillo, Land sale, Presidio of San Elizario, 2 March 1825, El Paso County Deed Book A, 241; José Antonio Arroyo to Joaquín Gándara, Possession of land, Puesto of San Elizario, 16 January 1826, El Paso County Deed Book A, 231; José Antonio Arroyo to José Ignacio Carrasco, Possession of land, Puesto of San Elizario, 16 September 1836, El Paso County Deed Book A, 229; José Nemesio Márquez to José Durán, Possession of land, Puesto of San Elizario, 10 May 1833, El Paso County Deed Book A, 310; Joaquín Gutiérrez to Juan Núñez, Possession of land, Puesto of San Elizario, 31 December 1834, El Paso County Deed Book A, 272.

3. Timmons, "El Paso Area," 2, 5.

4. Timmons, *El Paso*, 74.

5. Manuel Gómez Pedraza, Circular, Mexico City, 28 February 1825, AGN, Guerra y Marina, Impresos, Caja 64.

6. Guadalupe Victoria, Decree, 21 March 1826; and *Estado* showing the forces required by the five companies consid-ered necessary for garrisoning the State of Chihuahua (3 February 1826, AGN, Guerra y Marina, Impresos, Caja 21, exp. 10.)

7. José Antonio de Arce to the ayuntamiento of El Paso, 1 April 1823, JA I, r. 2, bk. 13, 1820–23, f. [90–91].

8. Griffen, *Utmost Good Faith*, 27.

9. José Agustín de Escudero, *Noticias estadísticas del Estado de Chihuahua* (Mexico City, 1834), 225.

10. Ibid., 233–34.

11. To date the degree of acculturation of the Apache colony of more than a thousand individuals living outside the walls of the San Elizario presidio remains unclear and requires further research. Unfortunately most of the sacramental records of Ysleta and Socorro, which might have provided some clues, at least regarding intermarriage between Hispanics and Apaches, were lost when flooding swept away the missions in 1830. Moreover, the marriage and burial books for San Elizario in the Spanish and Mexican periods are missing.

   Relying on such sacramental books to explore the subject of what the author calls "*mestizaje* (racial mixing)" between Hispanics and Apaches at the presidio of Junta de los Ríos, Jones concluded that "La Juntans acculturated and were indeed assimilated into the Spanish population." By contrast Griffen used presidial records from Janos to show that although Apaches were occasionally baptized there, or traded a horse with a Hispanic family, "there is no evidence that Apaches assimilated in groups in the Janos population." (Griffen, *Apaches*, 110, 268. Oakah L. Jones, "The Settlements and Settlers at La Junta de los Ríos, 1759–1822," *The Journal of Big Bend Studies* 3 [January

1991]: 58.)

12. Griffen, *Apaches*, 133. Griffen, *Utmost Good Faith*, 29.

13. Griffen, *Utmost Good Faith*, 30–32.

14. Timmons, "El Paso Area," 3; C. L. Sonnichsen, *The Mescalero Apaches* (Norman, 1958), 55.

15. Griffen, *Utmost Good Faith*, 164–65.

16. Urban cavalry company of San Elizario, November 1836, JA I, r. 6, bk. 33, 1836, vol. 4.

17. Janet Lecompte, *Rebellion in Río Arriba, 1837* (Albuquerque, 1985), 67–68, 72, 111. See Service Record of José Mízquiz in the Documentary Appendix, page 114.

18. Griffen, *Utmost Good Faith*, 56–58.

19. Timmons, *El Paso*, 79–80.

20. Moorhead, *Presidio*, 270.

21. Census of El Paso Area for 1833, JA I, r. 4, r. 144; Census of San Elizario, 1834, JA II, r. 27, bk. 2, 1834, f. 221–48.

22. Ronald Spores and Ross Hassig, eds., *Five Centuries of Law and Politics in Central Mexico* (Nashville, 1984), 154–59.

23. Gregorio Gándara to Joaquín Molina, Possession of land, Puesto of San Elizario, 6 April 1843, El Paso County Deed Book A, 274.

24. W. H. Timmons, Lucy F. West, Mary A. Sarber, eds., *Census of 1841 for Ysleta, Socorro, and San Elizario* (El Paso, 1988).

25. Griffen, *Utmost Good Faith*, 169–70.

26. Report of the towns of the El Paso district, 18 September 1840, JA I, r. 10, bk. 52, 1840, vol. 4, f. 223.

27. Documents related to the personal contribution imposed and collected for the expenses of the war against the Texan invasion. (1841, JA II, r. 31, bk. 1, 1841, f. 288–388.)

28. Timmons, *El Paso*, 86.

29. Ibid., 87.

30. Carlos María Bustamante, *El gabinete mexicano* (Mexico City, 1842), 2:3, 9, 216.

31. Griffen, *Utmost Good Faith*, 70–71.

32. Warren A. Beck, *New Mexico: A History of Four Centuries* (Norman, 1962), 128; Almada, *Resumen*, 215.

33. General Command, Inspection of the Department of Chihuahua, Chihuahua, 30 June 1843, AGN, Guerra y Marina, Caja 70.

34. General Command, Inspection of the Department of Chihuahua, Chihuahua, 31 May 1843, AGN, Guerra y Marina, Caja 70.

35. General Command, Inspection of the Department of New Mexico, Santa Fe, 12 December 1843, AGN, Guerra y Marina, Caja 70.

36. General Command, Inspection of the Department of Chihuahua, Chihuahua, 5 January 1844, AGN, Guerra y Marina, Caja 70.

37. Juan Bustamante, Funds given to presidial soldiers in El Paso, El Paso, 3 April 1844, MANM, r. 36, f. 745–46.

38. See, for example, Félix Lerma to Mariano Monterde, Santa Fe, 12 October 1844, MANM, r. 35. f. 335–36; Governor of New Mexico to Alferez Gaspar Ortiz, Santa Fe, 28 May 1845, MANM, r. 35, f. 725; Governor of New Mexico to the commandant of the Rural Company, Santa Fe, 30 October 1845, MANM, r. 38, f. 908; Félix Lerma, Certification of Baptism, San Elizario, 20 October 1843, AHAD–297, f. 751.

39. General census of the population of San Elizario, 25 January 1844, JA II, r. 33, bk. 1, 1844, f. 68–76.

40. Griffen, *Utmost Good Faith*, 97.

41. Military report of the towns of the El Paso district, 1845, JA II, r. 34, bk. 1, 1845, f. 428.

42. Military report of San Elizario, 31 May 1846, JA II, r. 35, f. 252–57.
43. Timmons, *El Paso*, 91–92.
44. Sebastián Bermúdez to the governor of Chihuahua, 25 August 1846, in José M. Ponce de León, ed., *Reseñas históricas del Estado de Chihuahua* (Chihuahua, 1910), 332–33; José Eligio Muñoz to the prefect of El Paso del Norte, 26 September 1846, JA I, r. 38, 1846, f. 125–26.
45. Timmons, *El Paso*, 93.
46. Ibid.
47. William Elsey Connelley, *Doniphan's Expedition* (Kansas City, Mo., 1907), 373–78.
48. Timmons, *El Paso*, 95; Stella M. Drumm, ed., *Down the Santa Fe Trail and into Mexico: The Diary of Susan Shelby Magoffin, 1846–1847* (Santa Fe, 1975), 211.
49. Ralph P. Bieber, ed., *Journal of a Soldier under Kearny and Doniphan by George Rutledge Gibson* (Philadelphia, 1974), 323–24; J. J. Bowden, *Spanish and Mexican Land Grants In the Chihuahuan Acquisition* (El Paso, 1971), 89.
50. Connelley, *Doniphan's Expedition*, 384.
51. Conkling and Conkling, *Butterfield Overland Mail*, 2:51–52.
52. Almada, *Resumen*, 225.
53. Timmons, *El Paso*, 98.
54. Timmons, "Presidio," 115; José Joaquín de Herrera, Decree, Mexico City, 25 June 1848, AGN, Guerra y Marina, Impresos, Caja 22, exp. 1848; Pedro María Anaya, Decree, Querétaro, 16 December 1847, AGN, Guerra y Marina, Impresos, Caja 64, exp. 661.

Chapter 4

1. In 1848 American officials argued that the southern channel was the deepest one and that therefore Ysleta, Socorro, and San Elizario were in United States territory. (Timmons, "El Paso in the Mexican Period," 24, 27.)
2. Ferol Egan, *The El Dorado Trail* (New York, 1970), 114–24.
3. Rex W. Strickland, *Six Who Came to El Paso—Pioneers of the 1840s*. Southwestern Studies 3 (El Paso, 1963), 5–10.
4. Chihuahuan protests against the terms of the Treaty of Guadalupe Hidalgo and forced removal of Mexican officials in the communities of Socorro, Ysleta, and San Elizario ran in the official state newspaper. ("Gobierno del Estado" and "Editorial," 23 January 1849; "Gobierno del Estado," 30 January 1849; and "Juan Pedro Pérez to the jefe político of Cantón Bravo, San Elizario, 12 January 1849." *El Faro, Periódico del Gobierno del Estado Libre de Chihuahua;* W. H. Timmons, "American El Paso: The Formative Years, 1848–1854," *Southwestern Historical Quarterly* 86 [July 1983]: 2–3.)
5. Timmons, "American El Paso," 3.
6. George P. Hammond and Edward H. Howes, eds., *Overland to California on the Southwestern Trail, 1849, Diary of Robert Eccleston* (Berkeley, 1950), 132–33.
7. Timmons, "American El Paso," 4.
8. Timmons, "Presidio of San Elizario," 113.
9. Ibid., 114.
10. Ibid., 115. Frederick Augustus Percy, a true son of Old England who visited San Elziario (his spelling) in 1854, wrote: "Many remnants of the extensive military barracks erected under the Spanish rule yet remain, and we are

informed by the old inhabitants of the place that within their recollection 5000 regular soldiers were stationed in the said place—we do not conceive this to be an exaggeration as the limits of the garrison enclosed by a wall yet remaining contains not less than 15 or 20 acres of ground." (Rex W. Strickland, ed., *El Paso in 1854* [El Paso, 1969], 16.)

11. Charles A. Hoppin to Peter H. Bell, 3 January 1850, Governors' Papers: Bell, Texas State Archives.

12. "Governor Bell's Message," 26 December 1849, published in the *State Gazette* (Austin), 29 December 1849; William Campbell Binkley, *The Expansionist Movement in Texas, 1836–1850* (Berkeley, 1925), 177.

13. Bell to the Senate, 3 January 1850, Governors' Papers: Bell, Texas State Archives.

14. "From El Paso," *State Gazette* (Austin), 27 April 1850; J. Morgan Broaddus, *The Legal Heritage of El Paso* (El Paso, 1963), 34.

15. Broaddus, *Legal Heritage*, 47, 52, 60–61.

16. John Russell Bartlett, *Personal Narrative of Explorations and Incidents in Texas, New Mexico, California, Sonora, and Chihuahua Connected with the United States and Mexican Boundary Commission During the Years 1850, '51, '52, and '53* (Chicago, 1965), 1:160–61.

17. William H. Emory, *Report on the United States and Mexican Boundary Survey* (Austin, 1987), 1:41.

18. Timmons, *El Paso*, 138.

19. Wayne R. Austerman, *Sharps Rifles and Spanish Mules: The San Antonio-El Paso Mail, 1851–1881* (College Station, Tex., 1985), 19–32.

20. Robert H. Thonhoff, *San Antonio Stage Lines, 1847–1881*; Southwestern Studies 29 (El Paso, 1971), 9–16; Austerman, *Sharps Rifles*, 69, 82; Nancy Hamilton, *Ben Dowell, El Paso's First Mayor*. Southwestern Studies 49 (El Paso, 1976), 21.

21. Lewis Burt Lesley, ed., *Uncle Sam's Camels—The Journal of May Humphreys Stacey Supplemented by the Report of Edward Fitzgerald Beale* (Cambridge, 1929), 170–71.

22. John C. Reid, *Reid's Tramp, Or a Journal of the Incidents of Ten Months' Travel Through Texas, New Mexico, Arizona, Sonora, and California* (Austin, 1935), 139–61.

23. Joseph Leach, "Stage Coach Through the Pass—The Butterfield Overland Mail Comes to El Paso," *Password* 3:4 (October 1958): 130–34. Waterman L. Ormsby, *The Butterfield Overland Mail by Waterman L. Ormsby, Only Through Passenger on the First Westbound Stage*, Lyle H. Wright and Josephine M. Bynum, eds. (San Marino, Calif., 1972), 77–78.

24. Anson Mills, *My Story* (Washington, D.C., 1918), 51–52.

25. Nancy Lee Hammons, *El Paso to 1900* (El Paso, 1983), 43–44; Rex W. Strickland, ed., *Forty Years at El Paso by W.W. Mills* (El Paso, 1962), 28.

26. Timmons, *El Paso*, 146–47.

27. Ibid.

28. Jerry D. Thompson, ed., *Westward the Texans* (El Paso, 1990), 32–33.

29. Jerry D. Thompson, *Henry Hopkins Sibley: Confederate General of the West* (Natchitoches, 1987), 187–90; Timmons, *El Paso*, 156. Lansing B. Bloom, ed., "Bourke on the Southwest," *New Mexico Historical Review* 13 (April 1938): 207.

30. Timmons, *El Paso*, 156.

31. Complaint of Ysleta citizens to Governor J.W. Throckmorton, 18 November 1866, Governors' Papers: Throckmorton, Texas State Archives.

32. List of Registered Voters, El Paso County, 1867–1869, Texas State Archives.

33. Mario T. García, *Desert Immigrants: The Mexicans of El Paso, 1880–1920* (New Haven, 1981), 156.

34. A. M. Gibson, *The Life and Death of Colonel Albert Jennings Fountain* (Norman, 1965), 53.

35. Ibid., 55.

36. Ibid., 55–56.

37. C. L. Sonnichsen, *Pass of the North* (El Paso, 1968), 186; Strickland, *W. W. Mills*, 146.

38. Sonnichsen, *Pass of the North*, 195–96.

39. Petition from Luis Cardis and Charles Howard to the Texas Legislature, San Elizario, 19 February, Memorials and Petitions, Texas State Archives.

40. Hammons, *El Paso*, 57, 81.

41. Bowden, *Spanish and Mexican Land Grants*, 157–58; Timmons, "Presidio of San Elizario," 114.

42. Bill Lockhart, "Gregorio Nacianceno García, 1st: Indian Fighter and Politician," *Password* 40:3 (Fall 1995): 119. García's age in 1841 was twenty-two, suggesting that he was born in 1819. (Timmons, West, and Sarber, *Census of 1841*, 88.)

43. Lockhart, "Gregorio Nacianceno García, 1st," 119–20; Minutes of the Corporation of the Town of El Paso, 1864–70, and United States Census for 1860, University of Texas at El Paso Library.

44. Sonnichsen, *Mescalero Apaches*, 113–33.

45. Broaddus, *Legal Heritage*, 91. For additional information on the Montes family, see Amelia Montes Skaggs and Dr. Samuel R. Skaggs, *The Bells of San Eli* (Las Cruces, n.d.), 46–57.

46. El Paso attorney Tom Diamond has recently argued that San Elizario has remained incorporated since the passage of the 1871 legislation and that its incorporation is merely dormant. (Larry Lee, "San Elizario hears call to establish first city council," *El Paso Herald-Post*, Friday, 28 February 1997, sec. B; Bill Lockhart, "Incorporations of San Elizario, Texas," *Password* 40:4 (Winter 1995): 170;. Bowden, *Spanish and Mexican Land Grants*, 158.)

47. See chapters 3–5 of C. L. Sonnichsen, *The El Paso Salt War of 1877* (El Paso, 1961).

48. Ibid.

49. Ibid.

50. Ibid.

51. Paul Larrazolo, *Octaviano A. Larrazolo: A Moment in New Mexico History* (New York, 1986), 30–42; Minutes of the Corporation of the Town of San Elizario, 1878; and United States Census for 1880, University of Texas at El Paso Library.

52. Bowden, *Spanish and Mexican Land Grants*, 159.

53. Sister M. Lilliana Owens, *Carlos M. Pinto, S.J.: Apostle of El Paso* (El Paso, 1951), 69.

54. Lockhart, "Incorporations of San Elizario," 170.

55. Lockhart, "Incorporations of San Elizario," 171. Oral histories gathered from former residents of San Elizario confirm that some people in San Elizario strongly opposed the coming of the railroad. See, for example, Humberto Sambrano

interview with Lois Stanford, El Paso, Texas, 23 August 1993, manuscript in author's possession.

56. Bowden, *Spanish and Mexican Land Grants*, 159.

57. Bill Lockhart, "Gregorio Nacianceno García, 2d: Lawman and Politician," *Password* 40:3 (Fall 1995): 126; Minutes of the Corporation of the Town of San Elizario, 1882–83, University of Texas at El Paso Library; Katherine H. White, *The Pueblo de Socorro Grant* (El Paso, 1984), 86, 92.

58. Minutes of the Corporation of the Town of San Elizario, 1881, University of Texas at El Paso Library; Larrazolo, *Larrazolo*, 40–42.

59. Larrazolo, with the support of El Paso's Democratic Ring, was elected district attorney, but in New Mexico became a Republican. (García, *Desert Immigrants*. Larrazolo, *Larrazolo*, 45–50.)

60. E. H. Antone, ed., *Portals at the Pass: El Paso Area Architecture to 1930* (El Paso, 1984), 7–9.

61. William M. Pierson to the assistant secretary of state, El Paso del Norte, 30 November 1872, Dispatches from United States Consuls in Ciudad Juárez (El Paso del Norte), 1850–1906, General Records of the Department of State, Record Group 59, National Archives. Helen Orndorff first published Consul Pierson's fascinating sketches of Lower Valley agricultural methods in her article, "The Development of Agriculture in the El Paso Valley—The Spanish Period," *Password* 5:4 (October 1960): 139–47. See also Alice White, "The Beginning and Development of Irrigation in the El Paso Valley," *Password* 2:4 (November 1957): 106–14.

62. Timmons, *El Paso*, 25–26; Alice White, "The Development of Irrigation in the City of El Paso," *Password* 4:1 (January 1959): 31.

63. White, "Development of Irrigation," 31–32.

64. Owen White, *Out of the Desert—The Historical Romance of El Paso* (El Paso, 1923), 185.

65. Helen Orndorff, "Agriculture in the El Paso Valley, 1870–1914," *Password* 12:3 (Fall 1967): 80. For details of the El Paso agricultural exhibit at the Dallas Fair in October 1888, see Hammons, *El Paso*, 63.

66. Orndorff, "Agriculture in the El Paso Valley, 1870–1914," 82–83.

67. White, "Development of Irrigation in the City of El Paso," 34–35.

68. Ibid., 37.

69. Ibid., 37–38.

70. Orndorff, "Agriculture in the El Paso Valley," 83.

71. Eugene O. Porter, "The Great Flood of 1897," *Password* 18:3 (Fall 1973): 95–103.

72. G.A. Martin, "Old San Elizario: Home of the Salt War and of the Finest Wines in the World," *El Paso Herald*, 9 June 1923; reprinted in *Voice of the Mexican Border*, January 1934, published in Marfa, Texas.

73. Porter, *San Elizario*, 52.

Works Cited

Archival Materials

Archivo General de Indias, Seville, Spain (AGI)
    Audiencia de Guadalajara
    Audiencia de México

Archivo General de la Nación, Mexico City, Mexico (AGN)
    Caja Matriz
    Guerra y Marina
    Oficio de Soria
    Provincias Internas

Archivo General de Simancas, Simancas, Spain (AGS)
    Guerra Moderna

National Archives, Washington, D.C.
    General Records of the Department of State

New Mexico State Records Center and Archives, Santa Fe, New Mexico
    Mexican Archives of New Mexico (MANM)
    Spanish Archives of New Mexico (SANM) II

Rio Grande Historical Collections, New Mexico State University Library
    Archivos Históricos del Arzobispado de Durango (microfilm), (AHAD)

Texas State Archives, Austin, Texas
    Governors' Papers
    Lists of Registered Voters
    Memorials and Petitions

University of Texas at El Paso Library
    Archives of the Archdiocese of Durango (microfilm)
    Catholic Archives of Texas (microfilm), (CAT)
        Diligencias matrimoniales
    El Paso County Deed Books
    Janos Collection (microfilm)
        Juárez Archive (microfilm), (JA I, first filming and JA II, second filming)
    Minutes of the Corporation of the Town of El Paso
    Minutes of the Corporation of the Town of San Elizario
    U.S. Census records

Other Works

Almada, Francisco R. *Resumen de historia del Estado de Chihuahua.* N.p.: Ediciones del Gobierno del Estado de Chihuahua, 1986.

Antone, E. H., ed. *Portals at the Pass: El Paso Area Architecture to 1930.* El Paso: El Paso Chapter, American Institute of Architects, 1984.

Austerman, Wayne R. *Sharps Rifles and Spanish Mules: The San Antonio–El Paso Mail, 1851–1881*. College Station, Tex.: Texas A & M Press, 1985.

Bannon, John Francis. *The Spanish Borderlands Frontier, 1513–1821*. New York: Holt, Rinehart and Winston, 1970.

Barnes, Thomas C., Thomas H. Naylor, and Charles W. Polzer. *Northern New Spain: A Research Guide*. Tucson: University of Arizona Press, 1981.

Bartlett, John Russell. *Personal Narrative of Explorations and Incidents in Texas, New Mexico, California, Sonora, and Chihuahua Connected with the United States and Mexican Boundary Commission During the Years 1850, '51, '52, and '53*. 2 vols. Chicago: Rio Grande Press, 1965.

Beck, Warren A. *New Mexico: A History of Four Centuries*. Norman: University of Oklahoma Press, 1942.

Bieber, Ralph P., ed. *Journal of a Soldier under Kearny and Doniphan, 1846–1847, by George Rutledge Gibson*. Southwest Historical Series 3. Glendale, Calif.: Arthur H. Clark Co., 1935.

Binkley, William Campbell. *The Expansionist Movement in Texas, 1836–1850*. Berkeley: University of California Press, 1925.

Bloom, Lansing B., ed. "Bourke on the Southwest." *New Mexico Historical Review* 13 (April 1938): 192–238.

Bowden, J. J. *Spanish and Mexican Land Grants In the Chihuahuan Acquisition*. El Paso: Texas Western Press, 1971.

Brinkerhoff, Sidney, and Odie B. Faulk, eds., *Lancers for the King*. Phoenix: Arizona Historical Foundation, 1965.

Broaddus, J. Morgan. *The Legal Heritage of El Paso*. El Paso: Texas Western Press, 1963.

The Catholic Encyclopedia. Edited by Charles G. Herbermann. 15 vols. New York: Encyclopedia Press, 1913–22.

Caughey, John Walton. *Bernardo de Gálvez in Louisiana, 1776–1783*. Berkeley: University of California Press, 1934.

Chavez, fray Angelico. *Origins of New Mexico Families: A Genealogy of the Spanish Colonial Period*. Santa Fe: Museum of New Mexico Press, 1992.

Conkling, Roscoe P., and Margaret B. Conkling. *The Butterfield Overland Mail, 1875–1869*. 3 vols. 1947. Reprint. San Marino, Calif.: The Huntington Library, 1972.

Connelley, William Elsey. *Doniphan's Expedition*. Topeka: Bryant and Douglas Co., 1907.

Cutter, Donald, ed. "An Anonymous Statistical Report of Nuevo México in 1765." *New Mexico Historical Review* 50 (October 1975): 347–52.

Diccionario de autoridades. Biblioteca Románica Española 5. 3 vols. 1726–37. Facs. ed. Madrid: Editorial Gredos, 1979.

Drumm, Stella M., ed. *Down the Santa Fe Trail and into Mexico: The Diary of Susan Shelby Magoffin, 1846–1847*. New Haven: Yale University Press, 1926.

Egan, Ferol. *The El Dorado Trail*. New York: McGraw Hill, 1970.

El Paso Herald–Post

Emory, William H. *Report on the United States and Mexican Boundary Survey*. 2 vols. Austin: Texas State Historical Society, 1987.

Escudero, José Agustín de. *Noticias estadísticas del Estado de Chihuahua*. Mexico City: En la Oficina del Puente del Palacio y Flamencos, núm. 1 por Juan Ojeda, 1834.

El Faro: Periódico del Gobierno del Estado Libre de Chihuahua.

Galván Rivera, Mariano. *Ordenanzas de tierras y aguas o sea formulario geométrico-judicial para la designación, establecimiento, mensura, amojonamiento y deslinde de las poblaciones y todas suertes de tierras, sitios, caballerías y criaderos de ganados mayores y menores y mercedes de aguas*. 4th ed. Mexico City: Librería del Portal Mercaderes, 1851.

Gálvez, Bernardo de. *Instructions for Governing the Interior Provinces of New Spain, 1786*. Ed. and trans. by Donald E. Worcester. Quivira Society Publications 12. Berkeley: Quivira Society, 1951.

García, Mario T. *Desert Immigrants: The Mexicans of El Paso, 1880–1920*. New Haven: Yale University Press, 1981.

Gerald, Rex E. *Spanish Presidios of the Late Eighteenth Century in Northern New Spain*. Santa Fe: Museum of New Mexico Press, 1968.

Gibson, A. M. *The Life and Death of Colonel Albert Jennings Fountain*. Norman: University of Oklahoma Press, 1965.

Griffen, William B. *Apaches at War and Peace: The Janos Presidio, 1750–1858*. Albuquerque: University of New Mexico Press, 1988.

——. "The Chiracahua Apache Population Resident at the Janos Presidio, 1792–1858." *Journal of the Southwest* 33 (Summer 1991): 151–99.

——. *Utmost Good Faith: Patterns of Apache-Mexican Hostilities in Northern Chihuahua Border Warfare, 1821–1848*. Albuquerque: University of New Mexico Press, 1988.

Hackett, Charles Wilson, ed. *Historical Documents relating to New Mexico, Nueva Vizcaya, and Approaches thereto, to 1773*. 3 vols. Washington, D.C.: Carniege Institute, 1923–27.

Hamilton, Nancy. *Ben Dowell, El Paso's First Mayor*. Southwestern Studies 49. El Paso: Texas Western Press, 1976.

Hammond, George P., and Edward H. Howes, eds. *Overland to California on the Southwestern Trail, 1849, Diary of Robert Eccleston*. Berkeley: University of California Press, 1950.

Hammons, Nancy Lee. *El Paso to 1900*. El Paso: University of Texas at El Paso, 1983.

Hendricks, Rick. "A Documentary History of San Elizario, Texas." In vol. 2 *Lower Valley History* of *El Valle Bajo: The Culture History of the Lower Rio Grande Valley of El Paso*. Edited by John A. Peterson and David O. Brown. Austin: Hicks and Company/Archaeological Research, Inc., 1994.

——. "Massacre in the Organ Mountains: The Death of Manuel Vidal de Lorca." *Password* 39:4 (Winter 1994): 165–77.

——. "A Muster of the Presidio of San Elizario in 1819." *Password* 39:3 (Fall 1994): 135–39.

——. "Presidio." In *Encyclopedia of Latin American History and Culture*. Edited by Barbara A. Tenenbaum. Macmillan Library Reference USA. 5 vols. New York: Scribner's, 1996.

——. "Santa María de las Caldas and the Hacienda de San Antonio: *Diligencias Matrimoniales* from the Lost Curacy, 1733–1739." *Nuestras Raíces* 6:3 (Fall 1994): 115–32.

——. "Santa María de las Caldas and the Hacienda de San Antonio: *Diligencias Matrimoniales* from the Lost Curacy, 1733–1739." *Nuestras Raíces* 7:2 (Summer 1995): 74–82.

——. "Spanish-Indian Relations in El Paso del Norte in the Early Eighteenth Century: The Rebellion of 1711." Paper read at sixty-first annual meeting of the Society for American Archaeology, New Orleans, 10–14 April 1996.

——. "Tabardillo: The 1764 Typhus Epidemic in the El Paso del Norte Area." *Password* 38:2 (Summer 1993): 55–64.

——. *Two Spanish Colonial Censuses of the El Paso Area: 1784 and 1787*. CAR Report 709. Las Cruces: Center for Anthropological Research, New Mexico State University, 1992.

Jackson, Donald, ed. *The Journal of Zebulon Pike*. Norman: University of Oklahoma Press, 1966.

John, Elizabeth A. H. "Spanish-Indian Relations in the Big Bend Region during the Eighteenth and Early Nineteenth Centuries." *The Journal of Big Bend Studies* 3 (January 1991): 71–80.

Jones, Oakah L. "Settlements and Settlers at La Junta de los Ríos, 1759–1822." *The Journal of Big Bend Studies* 3 (January 1991): 43–70.

Jordán, Fernando. *Crónica de un país bárbaro*. Chihuahua: Centro Librero La Prensa, 1975.

Kessell, John L. *Friars, Soldiers, and Reformers: Hispanic Arizona and the Sonora Mission Frontier, 1767–1856*. Tucson: University of Arizona Press, 1976.

Kessell, John L., and Rick Hendricks, eds. *By Force of Arms: The Journals of don Diego de Vargas, New Mexico, 1691–1693*. Albuquerque: University of New Mexico Press, 1992.

Kessell, John L., Rick Hendricks, and Meredith D. Dodge, eds. *To the Royal Crown Restored: The Journals of don Diego de Vargas, New Mexico, 1692–1694*. Albuquerque: University of New Mexico Press, 1995.

Kinnaird, Lawrence, ed. *The Frontiers of New Spain: Nicolás de Lafora's Description, 1766– 1768*. Berkeley: Quivira Society, 1958.

Larrazolo, Paul. *Octaviano A. Larrazolo: A Moment in New Mexico History*. New York: Carlton Press, 1986.

Leach, Joseph. "Stage Coach Through the Pass —The Butterfield Overland Mail Comes to El Paso." *Password* 3:4 (October 1958): 130–37.

Lecompte, Janet. *Rebellion in Río Arriba, 1837*. Albuquerque: University of New Mexico Press, 1985.

Lesley, Lewis Burt, ed. *Uncle Sam's Camels—The Journal of May Humphreys Stacey Supplemented by the Report of Edward Fitzgerald Beale*. Cambridge: Harvard University Press, 1929.

Lockhart, Bill. "Gregorio Nacianceno García, 1st: Indian Fighter and Politician." *Password* 40:3 (Fall 1995): 119–25.

———. "Gregorio Nacianceno García, 2d: Lawman and Politician." *Password* 40:3 (Fall 1995): 126–28.

———. "The Incorporations of San Elizario." *Password* 40:5 (Winter 1995): 169–77.

McLaughlin, Walter V., Jr. "First Book of Baptisms of Nuestra Señora de Guadalupe del Paso del Norte." M.A. thesis, Texas Western College, 1962.

Mandell, Gerald J. "Commercial Ties Between New Mexico and Parral, 1632 to 1682." Albuquerque, 1994. Typescript.

Martin, G. A. "Old San Elizario: Home of the Salt War and of the Finest Wines in the World," *El Paso Herald*, 9 June 1923. Reprinted in *Voice of the Mexican Border*, January 1934, Marfa, Texas.

Matson, Daniel S. and Albert H. Schroeder, eds. "Cordero's Description of the Apache—1796." *New Mexico Historical Review* 32 (October 1957): 335–56.

Mills, Anson. *My Story*. Washington, D.C.: Byron S. Adams, 1918.

Moorhead, Max L. *The Apache Frontier: Jacobo Ugarte and Spanish-Indian Relations in Northern New Spain, 1769–1791*. Norman: University of Oklahoma Press, 1968.

——. *New Mexico's Royal Road*. Norman: University of Oklahoma Press, 1958.

——. *The Presidio: Bastion of the Spanish Borderlands*. Norman: University of Oklahoma Press, 1991.

Navarro García, Luis. *Don José de Gálvez y la Comandancia General de las Provincias Internas del norte de Nueva España*. Seville: Escuela de Estudios Hispano-Americanos, 1964.

Ormsby, Waterman L. *The Butterfield Overland Mail by Waterman L. Ormsby, Only Through Passenger on the First Westbound Stage*. Edited by Lyle H. Wright and Josephine M. Bynum. San Marino, Calif.: The Huntington Library, 1972.

Orndorff, Helen. "Agriculture in the El Paso Valley, 1870–1914." *Password* 12:3 (Fall 1967): 74–89.

——. "The Development of Agriculture in the El Paso Valley—The Spanish Period." *Password* 5:4 (October 1960): 139–47.

Owens, Sister M. Lilliana. *Carlos M. Pinto, S.J.: Apostle of El Paso*. El Paso: Revista Católica Press, 1951.

Pino, Pedro Baptista. *The Exposition on the Province of New Mexico, 1812*. Trans. and ed. with an introduction by Adrian Bustamante and Marc Simmons. Albuquerque: University of New Mexico Press, 1995.

Ponce de León, José M., ed. *Reseñas históricas del Estado de Chihuahua*. Chihuahua: Imprenta del Gobierno, 1910.

Porter, Eugene O. *San Elizario: A History*. Austin: Jenkins Publishing Co., 1973.

——. "The Great Flood of 1897." *Password* 18:3 (Fall 1973): 95–103.

Reid, John C. *Reid's Tramp, Or a Journal of the Incidents of Ten Months' Travel Through Texas, New Mexico, Arizona, Sonora, and California*. Austin: The Steck Co., 1935.

Salazar, J. Richard. "Spanish-Indian Relations in New Mexico During the Term of Commandant General Pedro de Nava, 1790–1802." Research Paper 32. Guadalupita, N. Mex.: Center for Land Grant Studies, 1994.

Sambrano, Humberto. Interview with Lois Stanford, El Paso, Texas, 23 August 1993.

Santiago, Mark. *The Red Captain: The Life of Hugo O'Conor, Commandant Inspector of the Interior Provinces of New Spain*. Arizona Historical Society Museum Monograph 9. Tucson: Arizona Historical Society, 1994.

Skaggs, Amelia Montes, and Dr. Samuel R. Skaggs. *The Bells of San Eli*. Las Cruces: n.p., n.d.

Simmons, Marc. "Settlement Patterns and Village Plans in Colonial New Mexico." In *New Spain's Far Northern Frontier: Essays on Spain in the American West, 1540–1821*. Edited by David J. Weber. Albuquerque: University of New Mexico Press, 1979.

Sonnichsen, C. L. *The El Paso Salt War of 1877*. El Paso: Texas Western Press, 1961.

—. *The Mescalero Apaches*. Norman: University of Oklahoma Press, 1958.

—. *Pass of the North*. 2 vols. El Paso: Texas Western Press, 1968.

Spores, Ronald, and Ross Hassig, eds. *Five Centuries of Law and Politics in Central Mexico*. Publications in Anthropology 30. Nashville: Vanderbilt University, 1984.

State Gazette (Austin).

Strickland, Rex W. *Six Who Came to El Paso —Pioneers of the 1840s*. Southwestern Studies 3. El Paso: Texas Western Press, 1963.

—, ed. *El Paso in 1854*. El Paso: Carl Hertzog, 1969.

—, ed. *Forty Years at El Paso by W. W. Mills*. El Paso: Carl Hertzog, 1962.

Thompson, Jerry D. *Henry Hopkins Sibley: Confederate General of the West*. Natchitoches, Northwestern State University Press, La: 1987.

—, ed. *Westward the Texans*. El Paso: Texas Western Press, 1990.

Thomas, Alfred Barnaby. *Forgotten Frontiers: A Study of the Spanish Indian Policy of Don Juan Bautista de Anza, Governor of New Mexico, 1777–1787*. Norman: University of Oklahoma Press, 1969.

Thonhoff, Robert H. *San Antonio Stage Lines, 1847–1881*. Southwestern Studies 29. El Paso: Texas Western Press, 1971.

Thurston, Herbert, S. J., and Donald Attwater, eds. *Butler's Lives of the Saints*. New York: Kenedy, 1962.

Timmons, W. H. "American El Paso: The Formative Years, 1848–1854." *Southwestern Historical Quarterly* 86 (July 1983): 1–36.

—. *El Paso: A Borderlands History*. El Paso: Texas Western Press, 1990.

—. "The El Paso Area in the Mexican Period, 1821–1848." *Southwestern Historical Quarterly* 84 (July 1980): 1–28.

—. "The Presidio of San Elizario, 1789–1851." *Password* 33:3 (Fall 1988): 107–15.

Timmons, W. H., Lucy F. West, Mary A. Sarber, eds., *Census of 1841 for Ysleta, Socorro, and San Elizario*. El Paso: El Paso County Historical Commission, 1988.

Weber, David J. *The Spanish Frontier In North America*. New Haven: Yale University Press, 1992.

White, Alice. "The Beginning and Development of Irrigation in the El Paso Valley." *Password* 2:4 (November 1957): 106–14.

——. "The Development of Irrigation in the City of El Paso." *Password* 4:1 (January 1959): 31–38.

White, Katherine. *The Pueblo de Socorro Grant*. El Paso: Katherine Hope Huffman White Memorial Trust, 1986.

White, Owen. *Out of the Desert—The Historical Romance of El Paso*. El Paso: McMath Co., 1923.

Williams, Jack Stephen. "Architecture and Defense on the Military Frontier of Arizona, 1752–1856." Ph.D. diss., University of Arizona, 1991.

——. "Pedro de Nava's Instructions for Governing the Apache Establishments of Peace, 1791." Tucson, 1985. Typescript.

Worcester, Donald E. *The Apaches: Eagles of the Southwest*. Norman: University of Oklahoma Press, 1979.

INDEX